Praise for *Success in 5 Minute.*

"Just like a daily spiritual or motivatio
5 Minutes a Day" readings are full of information and inspiration. By investing just 5 minutes a day, one can achieve success at a higher level in business and life. Use it to help you create your bigger brighter future."

Linda McKissack
Author of "Hold" and "Presentation Mastery for Realtors", Speaker and Business Coach with 25 plus years experience in real estate

"I followed Karen's suggestions each morning for seven days. By day eight I was excited to keep up my new habits because I was getting results. It was fast, easy, and fun—like getting a present every morning. I couldn't wait to read the day's success tip while drinking my morning coffee. Karen's approach is easy to follow and I'm already seeing results in a week!"

Moira Lethbridge, M.Ed.
Trainer, coach, and creator of Take the Leap to Success™ coaching program

"Karen Briscoe is force to be reckoned with in the real estate world. She has been through so many ups and downs and has emerged victorious when so many other agents would have quit. This book is so needed in this industry!"

Pat Hiban
International best-selling author of *6 Steps to 7 Figures — A Real Estate Practitioner's Guide to Building Wealth and Creating Your Destiny*

"Karen shows you how to prioritize the important aspects of your business—and life. By doing one simple thing a day for 365 days, imagine where you can be in one year!"

Tony Giordano
Author of *'the social agent'* and Founder of www.Giordano.Global

"Every professional should take a few minutes every day to capture some of the knowledge and wisdom Karen delivers in *Success in 5 Minutes a Day*. Each of her daily vignettes offers a nugget or two of practical advice that have helped make her one of the most successful real estate agents in the country. It's a must-read."

Ron Cathell
Principal broker, Keller Williams Realty, McLean, Virginia

"If success was easy, we could all do it—and now, thanks to Karen, we can! In *Success in 5 Minutes a Day* she gives us the opportunity to pick up daily habits that will be the foundation of a growing business. Don't miss the chance for a great journey to financial freedom from the industry's biggest star!"

Liz Trocchio Smith
Founder and CEO, The Trocchio Advantage, LLC
Certified executive business coach, trusted advisor, corporate consultant, and best-selling author

Whether you are new or a seasoned professional, Karen Briscoe provides the tools for excellence. This book provides the keys; all you have to do is open it up!"

Amina Basic
CEO/team leader
Keller Williams McLean/Great Falls
#1 real estate company in the world
#1 real estate training company in the world
Certified John Maxwell teacher, trainer, coach, and speaker

COMMIT TO GET LEADS

SUCCESS

IN 5 MINUTES A DAY™

— 66 DAY CHALLENGE® —

KAREN BRISCOE

5
MINUTE PRESS

ISBN 978-1-936961-35-1

Success in 5 Minutes A Day™ is a Trademark of 5 Minute Press, LLC

5 Minute Success™ is a Trademark of 5 Minute Press, LLC

The 66 Day Challenge® mark is registered by Rellek Publishing Partners, Ltd. Timeless Truths, LLC

Books are available for special promotions and premiums.

For details, contact:

Special Markets
5 Minute Press
6820 Elm Street
McLean, VA 22101

E-mail: specialmarkets@5minutepress.com
Published by 5 Minute Press

Start today!

DEDICATION

This book is dedicated to:

My dad and mom, who were my first cheerleaders and role models of what success looks like.

My husband, Andy, who has encouraged me to achieve success in all areas of my life and work.

Our children, Drew and Callie, who have brought both joy and challenge to my life beyond what I ever dreamed possible.

And to you, the reader: Here's to your success!

Here's to your Success in Business and Life!

Karen Briscoe

TABLE OF CONTENTS

Introduction: Secrets to My Success

Success in 5 Minutes a Day: Breakfast of Champions

How *Success in 5 Minutes a Day* Can Help You Achieve Your Sweet Spot of Success

The Sweet Spot of Success is the overlap of three strategies: success thinking, success activities, and success vision.

SUCCESS IN BUSINESS AND LIFE = SUCCESS SWEET SPOT

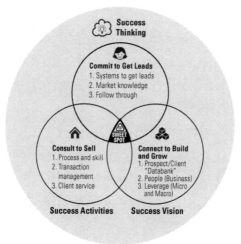

The Sweet Spot of Success is the intersection of all the best practices included in the *Success in 5 Minutes a Day* series. The possibilities and abilities are there all the time. It is by applying the principles of the model on a consistent basis, one day at a time, that a professional can best achieve the sweet spot of success.

Commit today to take the step every day to achieve the sweet spot of success in business and life.

Introduction
SECRETS TO MY SUCCESS

Hi, Karen here. Like many of us who become real estate agents, I entered the profession because I like people and houses and thought it would be a perfect combination. The scary part was that I didn't really want to be a salesperson. Immediately out of college I found myself in sales in the financial services industry (code for life insurance) and was honestly turned off by it, even though I was good at it. In order to be successful in sales, I had the perception that a person had to be pushy. Combine that with a strong fear of rejection, and looking back I still find it surprising that I was successful so quickly.

So what did I do to overcome my aversion to sales and rejection? My first secret was I embraced the approach of being helpful to people, to act as a consultant. In addition to having a strong head for business, I also have a heart for ministry. Instead of "selling" me and my services, I gave freely of my time and resources. I found that people were attracted to my low-key approach. To this day I embrace this philosophy—that the relationship needs to be win-win or no deal. I want people to work with me because they want to.

The next challenge I faced was how to let people know I was a real estate agent in such a way that they wouldn't feel like I was being "salesy." The old saying, "Don't be a secret agent," really hit home in real estate. So I started a database that included everyone I knew. I decided that if I added ten names each week, in one year I would have 520 contacts. That assured I was out meeting people, since I had to come up with ten names. This secret turned out to be a key aspect of success in sales of any kind! This was before e-mail and the Internet, so I chose the old-fashioned marketing platform of postcards. The postcards became conversation pieces in and of themselves, which made it easier for me to talk with people about real estate, because they brought up the subject!

This led to my secret of "touching" people. I tracked in a notebook everyone I talked to or wrote a note to about real estate (again, this was before the Internet and e-mail). Sometimes it was as simple as a birthday card and other times more complex, like a market study. I still have all those records, so I guess that this type of tracking is a secret of success too. My success activities consisted of touching twenty-five people every week or five people each "working day."

As more and more people found out I was in real estate, they would ask me about houses in their neighborhoods. True story: at a book club, one of my friends was better informed about a home in her neighborhood than I was. Boy, did I feel convicted. What kind of professional doesn't even know the product she is selling? That's when I discovered my next secret: know the inventory. A real estate agent is licensed to not only sell houses but also to see houses. So I started a systematic program to view houses, which I continue to do even today!

At this juncture I had reached a nice level of success, yet I felt there was more and I just didn't know how to achieve it. That's when I reached out to the best Realtor® I knew in the market. Sue Huckaby attended the same church as our family. Associating with a top agent was the secret of how I went from being a good agent to becoming a partner with Sue's top team in 2006.

Sadly, Sue passed away in September 2008, the same month that the financial markets crashed. Running the company alone was very hard in a very difficult market. After living in Texas in the 1980s during the savings and loan crisis, I had some experience with challenging real estate markets. My next secret was recognizing the market signs and quickly making the changes necessary to first survive and then thrive.

These changes included moving the team from a regional brokerage to Keller Williams International, which offered me a bigger platform to rebuild on. KW was and still is on the cutting edge in training and technology, key factors to being successful in this fast-changing business. At the same time, I focused on being lean, recognizing that I was operating a business and as such it had to make money. I worked hard to boost the bottom line. That meant cutting expenses such as heavy advertising, which was the backbone of the Sue Huckaby business, as well as making staff changes. No secret here—all of these were very hard decisions. And the market wasn't getting any better.

In 2009, Lizzy Conroy joined me as a partner. Lizzy was a past client and also a friend from church. She truly came along just in time, as I was becoming very discouraged operating the business alone. Thus, my next secret was that I recognized that I would rather be part of a team than a lone agent. The philosophy of "together everyone achieves more" really resonates with me. Lizzy is a fantastic partner with whom to share the triumphs and trials of running a business. Our partnership also allows each of us to have a life in addition to a business, which has been one of my best and greatest secrets.

The journey is much sweeter for me when it is shared. We are grateful to have an amazing support staff and the best agents around who work with our clients to provide top-notch service. And who could forget all the clients through the years whom we have served—many have become dear friends.

There are great rewards in achieving personal and professional success. I've found even greater rewards in helping others achieve success, which to me is the ultimate secret. It is similar to raising children—parents often cherish their children's accomplishments more than their own. It is the same when I coach and train an agent to success. It shows that my secrets to achieving success in real estate can be followed by others.

It leaves a legacy. Training, coaching, and inspiring agents to achieve their highest success is my gift.

So that brings me to this final secret: there are more secrets in the book! These stories are what I've been telling clients and agents throughout my career. They are "sticky" for a reason—you will be more likely to remember them. What good is an application or story if you never think of it again?

I hope you enjoy these secrets revealed by a top agent—me!

BREAKFAST OF CHAMPIONS

The advertising slogan "Breakfast of Champions," first made popular by Wheaties cereal in the 1930s, is about feeding your body healthy food to ensure top performance. I have found that the true breakfast of champions includes feeding your mind, as well.

Hal Elrod, author of *The Miracle Morning* series advocates reading each day as the fast track to transformation in one's life and business. Incorporate the habit of reading *Success in 5 Minutes a Day* for inspiration as part of your morning routine. Worldwide, countless, entrepreneurs, sales professionals, business owners and others have found you truly only have to invest five minutes a day to achieve amazing results. If they can do it—you can too!

Success in 5 Minutes a Day is transformative. The daily reader format contains memorable stories of information and inspiration. The messages are combined with a take-away to get into immediate action. Applied knowledge propels one to achieve success at a higher level.

The "*Commit to Get Leads*" *66-Day Challenge*® includes topics on: Systems to Get Leads; Market Knowledge and Follow Through. It is a key component of the entire program which incorporates topics on: Consult to Sell; Connect to Build and Grow; Success Thinking, Activities and Vision; all of which leads to the Sweet Spot of Success.

Yes, you too can achieve success at a higher level! Invest just 5 minutes a day to read "*Commit to Get Leads*" *66-Day Challenge*® to sharpen your knowledge, skills and abilities on lead generation. This one step will put you on the fast track. Start today!

Start today the habit of reading for inspiration and growth.

Apply the take-away to achieve a higher level of success in business and life.

DAY

1

HABITS AND 66 DAYS

Today marks the first day in your sixty-six journey of reading *Commit to Get Leads*. Sing the song "(Get Your Kicks on) Route 66" in celebration of the significance of the date. Studies have shown that it takes, on average, sixty-six days for a person to form a new habit.

People who achieve success in beginning a new habit or stopping an undesirable one go through a "habit loop." This is a three-part process, according to Charles Duhigg, author of *The Power of Habit*.

Days one to twenty-two mark the period when it is helpful to be an evangelist about your habit. Get out and tell people and solicit support. This creates the desire to complete the goal or risk embarrassment with friends and family. This process alerts your brain to focus on the behavior you want to make happen. During days twenty-two to forty-four, many people pause in self-reflection. Often people seek to understand the motivation and desire for wanting to create a positive habit or to stop a negative one.

The next period of days forty-four to sixty-six is when people start to experience burnout and might have difficulty sustaining the habit. Routine begins to kick in. Focus on the "light at the end of the tunnel" or at least catch glimpses of success and push through. During this stage, some people begin to experience the benefits of the new habit and the attributes of being in a "virtuous" cycle.

Day sixty-six is a milestone, one to celebrate. Get your kicks today on day sixty-six! Take a moment to circle back to those folks who supported you in the beginning and share the accomplishment. And if there were naysayers, call them, too—now they will be believers. The reward is key to putting the habit loop firmly in place.

Keep on keeping on. According to science writer David DiSalvo, it can take eighty days for a habit to become automatic: "Psychology research tells us that the average amount of time necessary to reach 'maximum automacity' (a habit) is sixty-six days. But when you are trying to develop a healthy habit, it's likely it will take eighty days for it to become automatic. The more complex the habit, the longer it takes to form."

Put the power of getting your kicks at day sixty-six with The 66 Day Challenge® Calendar available on the "5 Minute Success" website (under resources). Good habits, such as reading the books in the *Success in 5 Minutes a Day* series, are key to achieve and sustain long-term success.

———— ❧ ————

Celebrate today - establish empowering success habits!

DAY 2

THE FOUR PS OF MOTIVATION

There are primarily four forces that motivate people to make change, and conveniently they all happen to begin with the letter "P": push, pull, pain, and pleasure. Real estate agents are really change agents; we help people navigate the change of buying and selling a home and the process of moving. These four forces can occur in multiple combinations. For example, a "push" can occur at the same time as a circumstance that illicits "pain."

A "push" motivator is an event or factor that is "pushing" the person to move. Perhaps it is the loss of a job and the move is to economize. Another "push" example occurs when the next home has already been purchased and the seller does not want the expense of two mortgages.

The client feels the "pull" when there are circumstances that are pulling them to make a move. The "nesting" instinct when couples are expecting a child frequently creates a strong pull for purchasing a home. Another "pull" occurs at the other end of the real estate life cycle: that of the empty nester. People in this situation often feel pulled to a new life beyond that of raising children in a big house. Often this "pull" occurs around the same time as retirement, when moving to a warmer climate or somewhere with a lower cost of living is tugging at them.

"Pain" often occurs with a life event that is deemed negative at the time, such as divorce, death, loss of a job, or financial reversal. And "pleasure" in most cases is associated with joyful life events or circumstances, such as marriage, welcoming a child into the family, a new career, or financial abundance.

As mentioned, the driving forces almost always occur in some combination. A divorce pushes the family to sell the home, which is painful for everyone. And yet somewhere along the journey there is the pull of a new life and the pleasure of moving on.

Awareness is the first step I have found in understanding the four Ps. As a real estate agent, being cognizant of the factors motivating clients to make the move to buy or sell a home is how I can best meet their true needs. On the surface, it may seem as though it is just a financial and legal transaction, yet underneath there are multiple levels of emotion present.

Understand and use the four Ps of motivation to help your clients navigate change.

DAY 3

FEET ON THE STREET: KNOW THE INVENTORY

One of the primary responsibilities of salespeople is to know their product. Our son's first job during high school was at the local hardware store. One of his first tasks was to learn the location of all 40,000 items in the store. The store prided itself on customer service. When someone entered McLean Hardware and asked about an item, there was always a salesperson at the front to take him to the product. Once the product has been located, then the features and benefits were presented to the customer.

The same principle applies to other product sales. The shoe store salesperson must know what brands and styles of shoes are available in stock and by order. Professional software and financial service representatives stay knowledgeable of industry offerings to best meet their clients' situations. Office supply and food service vendors know the inventory available in order to serve their customers. Many companies offer "boot camps" and training programs to get new recruits up and running quickly on product knowledge. Professional salespeople and consultants upgrade their knowledge, skills, and abilities to stay abreast of new product lines and industry changes.

The real estate agent's products are homes and properties. With technology, one can view homes with a click of a button from the comfort of her office or on a smartphone or tablet. Yet nothing compares with actually going to see the property in person. It is feet-on-the-street observations gained from experience. The position of a home on the lot, what it backs up to, is across from, and the grade of the land are not always conveyed accurately in the Google Earth view and photos. Just doing a drive-by tells volumes about the nature of the neighborhood. Is it well-kept or experiencing decline, are there a lot of other homes for sale? Walking through a home conveys how well the home has been maintained: is there a good flow, and is the price in line with the market?

Another strong aspect of inventory knowledge involves prospecting for business. When viewing homes, a professional agent can use it as a time to think of people who might be in the market to buy the home. Further, if the agent happens to be conveniently in the neighborhood of people in her sphere or past clients, it is a great "warm" call or opportunity to pop by and touch base. Everyone wants to know what is going on in their neighborhoods and communities. In the call or visit, make the easy segue into inquiring if the neighbor happens to know of anyone in the market to buy or sell in the community.

The actual knowledge of inventory keeps the agent current on the market and comparables. This is particularly important when preparing the documentation that supports the contract value for the appraiser. It is the informed agent who best services her clients' real estate needs. There will always be business for real estate agents who are true neighborhood specialists and possess strong market expertise. Earn that distinction with "feet-on-the-street" knowledge of the inventory.

Preview houses to stay knowledgeable on inventory and for business development.

DAY 4

DATABASE IS YOUR DATABANK

Many people pass the real estate license requirements test and then are surprised to discover the world is not clamoring to hire them. In effect, the real estate agent has nothing to do until he has a lead.

Actually, this is true of other professions and businesses as well. Think of the doctor: there is no one to practice medicine "on" until the physician has a patient. In law, there are no means to practice the legal profession until one has a client. In a grocery store or a flower shop, until a customer arrives with a need to fill, there is no business to conduct. Lead generation is truly every person's job and opportunity.

One of the most common sources of business for a real estate agent is her sphere of influence (SOI). In the real estate profession, the SOI includes those people who would recognize the agent's name, known as a "strong" tie. There can actually be more social currency with someone who has a "weak tie." This phenomenon is documented by the Pew Research Center, according to executive and entrepreneur Kevin McKeown in "The Strength of Weak Ties in Social Networking: Seek to Be Worth Knowing."

The key to success is to engage with people, whether online or offline. Build a database of their contact information. This "databank" becomes the agent's source of current and future business.

There can be a lifecycle to a real estate business. At infancy, the agent is brand new to the profession. She toddles along the first few years, finally gaining a foothold and achieving success. Once past adolescence, she comes into her own and enters young adulthood with confidence. The databank is where the agent crosses over from being only as good as her last lead to that of a business owner. She continues to connect to build and grow the business through the middle-age years into maturity. As time passes, the agent plans for retirement. At this stage, many successful agents sell their past client and sphere list and earn a residual income. The databank has truly become an asset.

This is why one of the top priorities of professional agents is to treat the database as one would treat an investment account. It is a key to success to keep it current and to actively feed and grow this vital source of leads.

Take active steps to consistently build and grow your databank.

DAY
5

LEAD DOMINO EFFECT

The domino effect occurs after one knocks over the first domino in a string. The chain reaction that happens can lead to an extraordinary outcome. In the words of author BJ Thornton: "Every great change starts like falling dominoes." In real estate, every lead has the ability to start a chain of business opportunity that can achieve geometric results.

A number of years ago, my business partner took a sign call lead off a listing I had in McLean. That particular home did not work for her buyers, yet Lizzy was able to sell them a home in nearby Great Falls. This also meant they needed to sell their home in Vienna, which Lizzy represented as the listing agent. An agent on our team held Sunday open houses at the home a number of times. Out of those opens, he made the acquaintance of two couples that each purchased an upper-bracket home in Great Falls. For one of the groups, he sold their home in Herndon as the listing agent. This led to two referrals on the street, which also resulted in sales. And another of the open house attendees actually bought the home in Vienna. Additionally, I sold the original listing in McLean. This one lead set up several chains of domino reactions, resulting in almost $10 million in transactions within a couple years.

The challenge is that the agent doesn't necessary know which one of the dominoes is going to set off the chain reaction. Gary Keller, in *The One Thing,* uses this as the barometer to decide which domino to focus on: "What is the *one* thing you can do, such that by doing it everything else would be easier or unnecessary?" Consistent, proactive prospecting is the one way guaranteed to create opportunity in real estate. It is the lead that starts the domino effect for the successful agent.

This may be hard to believe, yet I have heard agents actually say that they would be overwhelmed if they had too many prospects. This is a position of amazing power and opportunity. Yes, the agent must take on the challenge of learning to manage the workflow. This is where the agent goes from being only as good as her next lead to connecting to build and grow a business. Options at this juncture include referring the lead out for a fee, partnering with other agents, and employing staff to assist. These are all good challenges!

Scientists project that the chain reaction of one two-inch tall domino, doubled each time, would stretch from the Earth to the moon by the fifty-seventh time. The geometric power of domino progression is a secret to success, which can be yours as well if you embrace it as part of your business development plan.

Employ the power of the domino effect to achieve extraordinary åresults in your business and life.

INVEST IN CLIENTS

One of the best investments that real estate agents can make is in their clients. Repeat business and referrals are the lifeblood of a professional's success. Just as one continues to invest in a financial portfolio every year, the investment into clients also pays long-term dividends.

A secret to my success early in my real estate career was creating a database of all the people in my community who would recognize my name. I realized there would be attrition to that list, so I committed to adding ten names each week. Just think: this one habit meant that my client list grew by 520 names every year!

Every time I met someone, whether on an official real estate appointment or just casually, I would update the database with the relevant information. It really makes people feel special when you remember their birthday and their kids' names. One of my earliest clients, whom I knew from church, called me when she wanted to purchase a home because she was so touched that I sent all the members of her family cards on special occasions.

On the real estate front, keeping detailed records of all conversations means that I can refer back to what was previously discussed, even if it occurred years ago. This reduces the chance of miscommunication. Further, it conveys that I care enough to keep track of what is going on with their situations.

Other agents ask if I put "everybody" in my database. My response is that I wouldn't purchase every stock on the stock market. So no, I don't. Consider your clients as your investment portfolio; your database should include those who will help you build and grow your business. The distinction is between being an advisor or just an order taker.

Financial counselors advise investing with a long-term perspective. Take that view with your client portfolio and I predict a long and successful career in real estate.

Invest in your clients today and every day for a strong real estate business portfolio.

DAY 7

COUNT YOUR LEADS AND MAKE YOUR LEADS COUNT

The idea of "counting your leads and making your leads count" comes from the classic Bing Crosby song, "Count Your Blessings." The message of the song is: "When you're worried and you can't sleep, just count your blessings instead of sheep; and you'll fall asleep counting your blessings." In the real estate profession, being commission-based means the source of all income is a lead. And then the lead must be converted into a sale before any income is earned. It can be a long process and in the interim many agents become worried, wondering where the money is going to come from. If this leads to lack of sleep, it can become a vicious cycle.

This is where I came up with the practice, personally and in our business, to "count your leads and make your leads count." By tracking every lead, the agent gets a better understanding of the sources of business. This brings clarity on what areas of lead generation are more productive. So when I become worried about where money is going to come from, I can razor-focus on the areas that have the best potential for return on investment for time and resources.

All leads contain within them the seeds of opportunity. Many times it is a situation for a buyer or seller of "not now." These leads are put into the pipeline and account for future business. Many agents focus primarily on high quality leads and if the customer doesn't seem to have urgency, they lose attention. With this practice, the agent loses the gold-mine opportunity of creating future business. This is where making every lead count has great merit for building a long-term lead-generation machine and growing a business. A benefit to strong tracking is that when an agent on the team is low on leads, she can go back and "mine" the ones that have been sitting on the sidelines. Maybe now is the time!

Many agents consider working with rentals as low-level leads. Yet if the agent truly recognizes that every lead contains a seed of opportunity, she will stay in touch with those tenants and convert them into buyers at some juncture. Landlords, too, can be potential sellers, either selling straight out or "buying up" to a higher income-producing property. The highest conversion I've personally experienced was a four-star general who rented for one year and then purchased a $2.8 million home. My business partner secured a rental for a dual doctor couple for several years and eventually sold them a new construction, $4.2 million home. Both are situations where we made the lead count rather than "looking down" on the short-term rental leads generated as not worth our time.

Set up a system for tracking leads to make every lead count today!

DAY 8

ACTIVITY BLOCKING

Many coaches and books on productivity recommend time blocking. This is where one sets aside a certain portion of time each day or week to generate leads or other key activities. Countless people find this means of accountability empowering. Others, though, "flitter away" the time and don't actually accomplish anything.

When our daughter was in elementary school, we discovered that she did not learn like other children. She had the great ability of appearing to be busy with homework and yet make no progress whatsoever in actually completing it. After paying numerous tutors to work with her, we still felt frustrated at the lack of progress. The sessions were set up for a specific time period, and when that time was up, she knew she could leave, even if the work wasn't completed. This is, to me, like time blocking.

Another tutor, who came highly recommended, held what she called "homework sessions." At these sessions, several students from different grade levels and skills met to complete their individual homework assignments. Everyone stayed until the work was completed, thus there was no incentive to use stalling tactics to put off doing the work.

Tutoring by several lead teachers was available during the homework sessions, as well as coaching by accomplished high school and college students. It provided an environment of group accountability as well—no one wanted to disappoint the other students in the program. On special occasions, if everyone was on target to complete their assignments, there would be a pizza party or other such event to look forward to.

Activity blocking is where a set number of completed activities are committed to for each day or week. Thus it is not time-bound, but rather completion-bound. One can "front load" the activities by working ahead if time off is scheduled. Also, "catching up" can occur if one falls behind. By tracking the activities, one can determine the results accordingly. Then an agent can project her goals and know what activities are necessary to reach those objectives.

Commit to completing a set number of activities each day and week for lead generation.

DAY
9

"REACH OUT AND TOUCH SOMEONE"

This advertising jingle, circa 1979, for AT&T is a great theme for real estate agents. The commercial series included mini movie-like vignettes about people reconnecting over a phone call. To achieve and sustain success as a real estate agent, a commitment to business development by "reaching out and touching someone" is an imperative.

In his book, *The Seven Levels of Communication*, Michael Maher illustrates the methods of communication in a pyramid. The base is advertising, next is direct mail, and above that is electronic communication. These three comprise the "informational zone"; that is, the sender delivers content that the recipient can choose to acknowledge or ignore fairly easily. Computers and hand-held devices offer e-mail for in-depth and potentially two-way communication. Social media and similar platforms provide ways to connect and stay in touch with clients, past clients, friends, and those in the agent's sphere of influence. Keep in mind that these methods often lack the personal touch and depth of emotion that a voice or personal touch can convey.

The next level of impact on the pyramid is handwritten notes. This is one of the key methods of communication I have used to great success. Many agents who work by referral also tout the effectiveness of this method to "reach out and touch someone" in a way that commands attention.

The top three levels of communication are: phone calls, events and seminars, and one-on-one meetings. These three make up the "influential zone" of impact, according to Maher.

Even with the advances in technology in the last decades, the telephone is still one of the best means of communication. With Skype and FaceTime, people can now view each other over a screen, just as depicted years ago in the *Jetson's* cartoons. For most people, a cell phone or smartphone is their primary number. It offers the option to text for quick and easy messages.

The top two levels of touching someone are literally in person, face-to-face, belly-to belly. Group opportunities include seminars, networking, and open houses. One-on-one connections in the real estate world can be scheduled appointments, showing homes, knocking on doors, or dropping by. There is something special about giving someone your time and personal attention. And it is important to truly be there and avoid distractions by turning off your phone!

No matter what the method, it is a high priority for real estate agents to reach out and connect with people on a daily basis. As American industrialist Henry Ford said: "You can't build a reputation on what you're going to do." The successful agent builds a reputation by "reaching out and touching someone."

Employ all levels of communication to "reach out and touch someone" to connect, and build and grow your business.

DAY
10

FILL THE PIPELINE

In sales jargon, to "fill the pipeline" and "keep the pipeline full" means to have business somewhere in the process that will lead to earned income. It goes without saying that a prospect or customer must be converted to a client in order to be able to move it along in the queue. Thus, the first order of business for all salespeople is to generate leads.

There are many methods and styles of prospecting. To keep a steady input, an agent should systematically, with no variance in schedule, actively solicit leads. Those agents who develop daily habits are the most likely to sustain long-term success. James Clear, author of *Transform Your Habits*, states: "The quickest way to build a new habit into your life is to stack it on top of a current habit." My prospecting habit is to "touch" five people each day. Early in my career, I attached that process with the new habit of tracking the touches in a spiral-bound notebook. This act creates a self-accountability loop, as well as gives me the satisfaction of knowing when I have done my five for the day.

The successful agent determines the amount of prospecting necessary in order to sustain current production. This is best achieved by creating and following a tracking system. To succeed to the next level requires stepping up activities known to lead to new business.

Invariably life happens along the way, as it should. For real estate professionals, in addition to the core responsibility of keeping the pipeline full of leads, most also handle other key functions: marketing, listing and buyer consultations, showing homes, contract negotiations including managing inspections and other contingencies, as well as the actual settlement process. All of these are part of the process of moving clients along through the pipeline so that at the other end there is an output of earnings for the agent.

In addition, there are cycles to the business and seasonal fluctuations to manage. So how does an agent do it all? One strategy is to "front load" prospecting. In anticipation of a busy time of the year, a vacation, or being out of the office for training for an extended period of time, an agent will "front load." This means conducting work ahead of schedule such that more lead generation occurs than is in the business plan.

Another strategy is to "back fill." In construction that term literally means to fill back in the material that was taken out. In this context, it means to fill the hole in the lead-generation plan that the agent has not yet completed. Runners use this concept when training for a marathon. If they miss a day running, they make it up on the weekend or go for a longer run a few days in a row.

True professionals follow good habits to do the work and are committed to lead generation.

***

Establish daily habits to keep the pipeline full.
Track, back fill, and front load as necessary.

DAY

FOLLOW-THROUGH

The expression to "follow up" is common in the language of sales, as when a salesperson says she will follow up on a lead. However, I have found that "follow-through" is what gets the job done. Follow-through is a principle in sports, particularly golf, in which the athlete continues the stroke or swing through to completion and in the direction of the desired outcome. The golfer lines up the stroke to the hole, beginning above the ball. The backswing that occurs prior to contact gives the club the momentum required to propel the ball into the air. If the athlete were to "pull up" or stop the swing short in some fashion, then the success of hitting the ball in the desired direction is unlikely.

Follow-through in real estate sales has similar principles. The sales agent often begins the effort prior to making contact with the customer. An example is that many agents use open houses as a means of prospecting. Just showing up at the designated time and putting signs out does not fully leverage the opportunity. The preparation that an agent performs prior to the event increases the likelihood of meaningful conversations and connections to occur at the open house. This is analogous to the "backswing," the effort that propels the ball forward. These activities can include viewing comparable homes on the market in the neighborhood and surrounding communities; preparing market studies and information to have available for open house visitors; inviting the neighbors to visit; and previewing the home and becoming familiar with the attributes, features, and upgrades.

After the open house and contacts have been made, then the agent has countless opportunities to connect with the leads. Meaningful follow-through includes thanking all attendees by e-mail, a phone call, or handwritten note; providing answers to inquiries made; sending further market studies as relevant; and doing research on neighboring communities that might be a better fit for the customer.

Follow-through activities for lead conversion have taken place once the customer has become a client. The next follow-through process includes the listing agreement through to contract to settlement for sellers and buyer agreement through contract to closing for buyers. The professional athlete and real estate agent truly never stop following through! This is because another correlation to sports is that both require practice in order to perfect the craft and skill. Professional golfers spend about three to four hours every day concentrating on their full swing and an equal amount of time on their short game. Successful real agents follow a similar schedule for prospecting and conversion to sell after winning the business.

Conduct follow-through activities for both prospecting and selling conversion.

DAY 12

DON'T BREAK THE CHAIN

Story has it that Jerry Seinfeld designed a self-motivating technique for writing his comedy show routines that became known as "Don't break the chain." A key to success for him was to consistently create new material. He found that just the act of writing improved his writing. For Seinfeld, time on task was the key to creating better jokes. The challenge was accountability. So he used a physical calendar and would literally mark off the day with a big red "X" when the task was accomplished. The long-term objective was to not break the chain, which became another level of motivation for him. Very simply, Jerry's process was to repeat an activity every day and by doing so achieve success.

This idea has numerous applications to life. Some examples that come to mind are exercise, reading something inspirational or newsworthy, calling or touching base with a loved one or friend, and eating for good health. There are apps available that one can use to track these activities, or one can do it the old-fashioned way and use a paper calendar like Jerry is purported to do.

For a real estate agent, some daily habits that lead to success are touching base with five past clients or those in one's sphere each day, previewing or showing three houses each day, and entering ten people into a database each day.

Reading the book *Success in 5 Minutes a Day* also follows this basic principle. A key to success is to perform productive habits every day.

One way to do so is to keep true to Jerry Seinfeld's mantra: "Don't break the chain."

Use the "don't break the chain" motivational technique to hold yourself accountable.

DAY 13

COMMIT TO LEAD GENERATION

You have a choice. It has been proven without a doubt that real estate agents who enjoy a long-term successful career are those who generate leads in a consistent manner. How do they do that? I believe the answer lies in the words of Jon Congdon: "Trade in the concept of staying motivated and replace it with commitment."

Failure is inevitable for those who only make a half-hearted effort. Much like a speed governor on a car, the full power and potential of the engine is not realized. This is why agents usually don't reach their full potential. First the agents have to remove what holds them back and next implement the habits to take their business to the next level, which involves commitment.

The reality is that without proactive effort, almost everything is in a state of deterioration or decline. As a listing agent, the majority of one's clients are sellers, which means they move. In my business, about one-half of seller clients every year move out of the area, which means they are not likely to become repeat clients. Yes, of course there is the potential for referrals and the opportunity to market to the neighbors. The point is that it requires the constant replacement of the pool of past clients with new customers.

Commitment, on the other hand, is a proactive stance. People who are committed stay on task even when they don't feel like it and even when it is difficult. That's the difference between commitment and motivation. If the agent requires internal or external motivation prior to acting, then the business is at the risk of the whims of the day.

How can agents develop commitment? First, decide that it is the priority and complete it first before shiny objects or interesting projects distract your focus. Next, establish habitual routines that consistently enforce commitment. Follow the "smart" rule: specific, measurable, attainable, realistic, and timely. If stuck, try some new techniques or tools to break through to the next level of success.

One technique I follow is that every Monday I determine how many days that week I establish as "working." Next, I set up on my smartphone calendar how many houses I plan to view that week. As I see houses, 1 update the list with the street address for the property. I plan as well for the number of prospecting touches I plan to make for that week. This way the "space" to accomplish these tasks is committed to on my calendar and in my mind. Then all I have to do is go back and fulfill it with the action.

There are smartphone apps and computer programs designed to facilitate the process. One of the secrets to success is the consistent commitment to productive habits.

Commit to consistent proactive lead generation by establishing "smart" habits.

PROSPECTING FROM A TO Z

There are occasions when agents literally get stuck and don't know where to begin to prospect. Who should they call first and how often? This paralysis actually can happen to me too, as I have countless people to follow up with, including past clients and sphere of influence, as well as warm and cold leads. This is a wonderful position to be in. The challenge becomes whom should I contact first? In order to make progress, I came up with a system to easily and quickly decide which lead to pay attention to first.

Every time someone makes a real estate inquiry or visits with me about listing their home, I prepare a file folder. My business partner, Lizzy Conroy, keeps her leads in a spreadsheet. Notes and information related to the real estate and the people involved are logged in both the file and in a database. This data dump clears my head so I am able to focus on the task that is in front of me without fear that I may forget something important.

The monthly calendar lines up fairly closely to the same number of letters in the alphabet. Voilá! A built-in system to prospect the leads, literally from A to Z. On the first day of the month I contact those people whose last name begins with "A." The second day of the month I call "B" prospects, and so forth. It works even when calling warm or cold leads.

True, there is not an exact match; some of the letters, such as "X," may not have many surnames associated with it. In those cases, I just do a bit of combining, similar to how a phone pad has WXYZ on the number 9 button. Another minor tweak is the reverse concept. Some of the letters, such as "M" and "T," are the first letter for many surnames. Since in all cases there are more days in the month than there are letters in the alphabet, I use those days to circle back and enjoy the opportunity to pick who to call at random.

What about the agent whose program to generate leads is based on business days? This just requires a bit of a work-around. For example, in 2016 the first day of the month fell during the workweek ten times and only twice on the weekends. Following this program, the agent will progress through the alphabet of contacts three or four times per year. An agent can still touch base with past key customers and her sphere several times per year by working only business days. The idea is to use the program as a tool for success.

The technique is a simple application to improve the consistency of an agent's business development. Everyone has contacts in their phones, databases, and e-mail lists. Use the A-to-Z lead-generation method to connect with people on a regular basis to achieve long-term success.

Incorporate prospecting from A to Z to achieve success in your real estate business.

DAY 15

START AT THE VERY BEGINNING

"Let's start at the very beginning, it's a very good place to start" are lyrics of the song "Do-Re-Mi" that Maria and the children sing in the movie *The Sound of Music*. Maria begins to sing and the children chime in. She teaches the fundamentals of music and once they know those, then all they have to do is mix them up to sing a "million different tunes."

Often real estate agents just don't know where to start. And so I say the same as Maria: "Let's start at the very beginning," which is lead generation. The fundamentals of prospecting are like the notes Do-Re-Mi-Fa-So and so on.

Consider "Do" as a customer lead. It's interesting to note that "do" has another meaning when used in a different context. To take action means to "do" something. Once a real estate agent has a customer or client lead, then the agent has something to "do."

"Re" could be the houses that are in the same neighborhood of the lead, which the agent could preview and find out more about. This leads to "Mi," which could be to delve deeper to find out more about the customer's situation. "Fa" could be the agent finding ways to be of service to clients to meet the needs of their particular circumstances. "So" is the follow-through involved. This includes developing a strategy on how to stay in touch and adding the lead to a database for follow up. "So"—what are you going to do as an agent to take this business opportunity to the next level?

Just as in the song, these steps in the process are the tools an agent can use to build a business. Once you know them well, creatively mix them up to find a million different ways to build a business through lead generation.

"Do" the activities today to generate leads and build a business.

VELCRO® IS STICKY

The inspiration for the fastening device Velcro® occurred when the inventor was hiking in the woods. He became frustrated by burrs that stuck to his clothing with a tenacity that made them difficult to remove. The secret to the product is that one piece has multiple tiny hooks that attach to the other piece of material that has "mating" loops. This design creates such a strong force that the two pieces can be pulled apart, yet retain their original form. The first applications were in clothing and since have gone on to be used by NASA and other industries. Think about the ways that the Velcro® concept applies to the real estate business.

What first comes to mind is lead generation. The more touches the agent has with a potential buyer or seller customer via marketing and prospecting activities, the more likely that person will convert to a client relationship. This is based on the sales principle that 80 percent of sales are made after the fifth to twelfth contact, according to the National Sales Executive Association. Thus, multiple hooks increase the connection with prospects. The process creates stickiness, so that the agent is top of mind when the buyer or seller is ready to make the decision to move or to make a referral.

The next example applies to the process of a client actually buying or selling a home. Although it is possible for buyers to purchase the first home they see, typically it is a more involved process. In most cases, the agent conducts a thorough buyer needs-and-wants analysis. Then the agent shows the client multiple homes before a decision is made.

On the seller side, very rarely does the first buyer who views a home write and present an offer. More common is that the agent engages in extensive marketing efforts to generate multiple potential purchasers to view the home. These processes contain countless steps to fasten the parties together. The more connections made between the parties, the securer the engagement is and the greater the commitment.

To build and grow a business, the agent who achieves and sustains success does so with multiple clients and numerous transactions over time and in the pipeline. This process has a greater potential for success than the agent who is only as good as her next deal. In these and other ways, applying the Velcro® effect is a more sustainable business model.

***

Apply the Velcro® sticky principle to clients and your real estate business.

CAREER BASEBALL PLAYERS' AT-BAT STATS

In professional baseball, the top career batting average is held by Ty Cobb at .366. In order to be considered in the rankings, a player has to have been at bat in at least 1,000 games. The top 178 baseball players rank between .300 to .366. The remaining 822 players' batting averages fall between .264 and .299. These statistics show what it takes to be a top baseball player. Ted Williams, ranked #6, once commented that those players who fail "only" seven times out of ten attempts will be the greatest in the game.

The same statistic holds true with top professional real estate agents. For every three listing appointments, one seller will become a client and the home will sell. One seller will select another real estate agent and the home will sell. The final seller will decide not to do anything at the time. So with this "at-bat" experience, the best agents "win" one listing out of every three opportunities.

There are a couple of strategies that are known to yield a higher "at-bat" ratio; both include the agent staying in touch with the customer. Thus, when ready to make the move, the customer remembers you.

These scenarios have played out over and over in my business. One such example is a seller that I met with more than ten years ago about listing his home for sale. As is typical for our market area, the seller interviewed three top agents. It wasn't the right time for him then, yet I continued to touch base faithfully a couple times every year over the course of the following decade. When finally ready to sell, this customer shared with me that he didn't even consider another agent this time around. I was the only professional that by perseverance showed I really wanted his business. That is the kind of diligence that he wanted in the sale of his home.

Another example is one in which I interviewed for a listing and wasn't selected. The other agent made promises about market value that I didn't feel would be achievable. When after nine months the home didn't sell, I touched base with the customer after receiving the alert that the listing had been withdrawn. The customer was impressed that I was aware of her situation and was ready to listen to the guidance I provided about the current state of the market. This time around she was ready to price correctly for the market and the home sold in a reasonable period of time.

It is important for baseball players to know their statistics. It is just as important for the real estate professional to track hers. If you are batting .333, then be happy—you are among the best in the industry!

***

Track your annual statistics for success—listings taken and sold versus appointments.

"WHERE EVERYBODY KNOWS YOUR NAME"

"Where Everybody Knows Your Name" is the memorable theme song to the 1980's hit television comedy series *Cheers*. This is a great theme song for real estate agents too. Remembering a person's name is one of the greatest compliments you can subtly give. There are numerous mnemonic devices for committing a person's name to memory.

One is the use of a physical location as a way to "tag" the person with that location. This provides a much "richer" memory source surrounding the person, which aids in recall. Usually recommended is to use a familiar location, such as one's kitchen or living room. What has worked for me is to use the customer's actual home. When introduced, ask the person where he lives. As a real estate agent with familiarity of the community, this is a quick way to associate the person's name with a neighborhood. The conversation can be richer if you know people who live in the neighborhood and make immediate connections. This also works as a great conversation starter. It enables you to introduce your profession as a real estate agent in a soft-sell manner.

Another way is to do a quick Internet search on the person as soon as you can. Numerous search resources abound: Google, Facebook, and LinkedIn are the primary ones I use. This enables me to see if we know any of the same people. Also, I can sometimes find a little bit more about them, their profession, where they are from, and where they currently live. Hobbies and interests often are displayed, which can make for excellent connecting conversations.

At a public real estate open house, agents often ask visitors to sign in on a guest register. Many times, attendees do not use the most legible handwriting. This is an opportunity to request gently that they spell their name for you. Some agents have found that digital sign-in programs make it more likely that people will "spell" their names correctly. Use this as an opportunity to find out something about people that can help you remember their names.

These words in the song are helpful to remember when hosting an open house: "There's one place in the world, where everybody knows your name, and they're always glad you came."

Establish the habit of knowing everybody's name.

PLANT THE SEEDS

In a lot of ways, a real estate agent is like a farmer. In fact, the process of business development in a geographic location is commonly known as "farming." The business tends to have a seasonal nature to it, as well.

The springtime is when a number of homes go on the market, which for the real estate agent is a time to plant the seeds of business. The fall often can be a time of harvest—the sale and settlement of the business. In the summertime, the agent focuses on the watering and nurturing of clients, including proactive weeding by providing service. Tending to clients includes fending off pests to make sure the seeds have a chance to come to fruition. The hot summer months require labor that isn't for the faint of heart. In the winter months, the agent prepares the soil, her sphere of influence and past clients. It is then ripe for spring planting right around the corner.

The illustration is meant to be figurative, as every season for the professional agent requires her to plant, tend, nurture, harvest, and prepare for the cycle to occur again. Every season has a lesson to be learned in order to achieve a more bountiful harvest. An area of focus is to increase the quality and quantity of the seeds that are planted.

In Ecclesiastes 11:4, it is written: "Farmers who wait for perfect weather never plant. If they watch every cloud, they never harvest." This means that the agent should not wait for a perfect market. It means he should not be discouraged by every difficulty that comes along. He should do the work regardless of the outcome. It is those agents who take action who are successful in spite of the market and the difficulties.

The amazing thing about planting real estate seeds is that one seed can lead to a bountiful harvest or multiple opportunities. An example was a Sunday afternoon when I was out viewing homes at public opens. It is part of my weekly soil-tending to keep current on the market. Little did I realize that I had walked into what effectively was a FSBO (for sale by owner). As a commercial broker, he decided because of his license to sell his own home. We chatted for a few minutes and I casually said that if he decided he was tired of doing it himself and wanted a professional, full-time agent to do the work for him, to give me a call.

The seed I planted in his mind took hold and a couple weeks later he did call me. I sold that $1 million home. Yet that's not all! He referred me to his neighbor; I sold his $1.7 million home and an $800,000 investment property. The original client called me a few years later and I sold his $2.4 million home when he decided to downsize. The buyers of the original home contacted me too, as they were impressed with the way I represented the seller side and hired me as their agent. I sold that home again for $1.1 million and sold them a $1.6 million home. That one seed led to a harvest of around $8.6 million worth of business. All of that bounty came from one seed.

Plant the seeds. Tend, nurture, harvest, and prepare to build and grow your business.

KEEP YOUR EYE ON THE PRIZE

When a kid opens up a box of Cracker Jacks™, what do you think he goes for first? The prize! It would be totally out of character for a child to eat the caramel-coated popcorn and peanuts one by one, patiently waiting until the prize appeared at the bottom of the box. The same hunger and desire for the prize, the fire in the belly, is the level of urgency with which professional real estate agents should view lead generation. She wakes up every morning with lead generation as her top priority.

What does this look like in reality? It means that prospecting activities take precedence over reading and answering routine e-mails. It means calling past clients and others in her sphere of influence until the agent has scheduled the requisite number of appointments for the week. It means delegating transactional-management responsibilities to other parties whenever possible.

The biggest shift occurred for me when it became an automatic process. I set up my routines and habits such that business development is the focus. That way I don't have to think about what I am going to do first and inadvertently get distracted by other shiny objects or activities.

The agent who is successful over time generates leads with the enthusiasm and drive of a kid who has just been given a box of Cracker Jacks™. He is a "crackerjack" real estate agent: a person of marked excellence.

The agent's enthusiasm influences buyers and sellers to take action. In the words of author and speaker Eleanor Doan: "You cannot kindle a fire in any other heart until it is burning within your own."

Be a "cracker jack" agent and keep the eye on the prize— lead generation is your priority today!

PEDAL TO THE METAL

Job one for the professional real estate agent is to prospect for clients. Until there is a lead, the agent truly has nothing to do. This situation applies to other professions and industries as well. Lawyers and CPAs call their leads clients, doctors and dentists refer to them as patients, churches refer to them as parishioners, and the hospitality industry knows them as guests or visitors.

Once an agent has either a buyer or seller client to work with, then all too typically the agent pulls his foot off of the accelerator or stops lead generating all together. The reason often is that he gets busy selling the client and the processing of the transaction to settlement, which are no doubt important tasks as well. Yet the distinction between those agents who sustain success year after year and those who experience great variance in their business cycles is the consistency of prospecting.

The reason is that once the momentum is achieved in anything, then it is much easier to sustain. Letting up on the gas can slow down the engine to a point that it requires maximum effort to regain the speed once had. Gary Keller, founder of Keller Williams, in his book, *The Millionaire Real Estate Agent,* states: "Nothing is more important to your sales career than prospective buyers and sellers."

It is also tempting to put the process on cruise control. Cruise control on a car still requires a thinking person, even though some features are available that are precursors to self-driving cars. The danger of cruise control is complacency. The engine maintains speed, yet still requires someone in control behind the wheel in order to navigate a detour up ahead. Another scenario is when the car is dangerously close to veering off the road or into traffic. The corollaries to a real estate agent's business are if the market shifts and one should "step on the gas" to get ahead or take the business in another direction. Or if the lead-generation method on cruise control is being derailed because that market niche has changed significantly, such as before and after the era of short sales and bank foreclosures.

There are some agents who take their foot off the accelerator in fear that there will be too many leads. Should that occur, it is an opportunity to leverage, delegate, and apply management skills. When there is more business than the agent can handle, options include referring out the business and other top-grade opportunities.

Putting the "pedal to the metal" is action that has urgency; it is a verb. Lead generation will always be top priority in the professional real estate agent's business.

---

*Keep the "pedal to the metal" in your
lead-generation activities!*

DAY 22

CATCH BUYERS AND SELLERS WHEN YOU CAN!

The movie *Catch Me If You Can* is an American crime drama based on a true story. The title reminds me that real estate agents should seek to catch buyers and sellers when they can! In order to be selected, an agent needs to be easily found and top of mind.

Houses are, in most cases, the most expensive asset people acquire and sell. Due to that reason, many customers choose to work with a trusted advisor to assist in the process. A common source is a referral from someone who has had personal experience with the agent.

Sources of recommendations can be from friends, relatives, associates, and neighbors (FRAN). This is an easy acronym to remember. The objective for the agent is to be front of mind so when someone expresses a real estate need, a referral will take place.

Another strategy many customers employ is to determine which real estate agents have been successful in the area. Past performance is no guarantee of future results, yet it is the best likelihood. An agent who has worked in the community knows the value of the location, the model of the home, and the neighborhood attributes. Along the same lines, real estate agents who live in a community often have a vested interest to provide top-notch customer service and keep prices strong. Many agents meet customers by being involved in the community through chambers, faith-based organizations, children's schools, arts and theatre programs, and volunteer organizations.

There are numerous marketing efforts that an agent can pursue to be well known in a community. She can host public and neighborhood open houses. She can knock on doors in order to meet the homeowners and sometimes renters who may be in the market to buy soon. Postcards that announce "just listed" and "just sold," newsletters, and market studies are all marketing pieces that capture attention and demonstrate that the agent is a producer.

Then there are the customers who start their search online. One of the agents on our team secured a listing because the sellers saw a blog about the neighborhood on our website. The sellers searched for agents who were familiar with that community and found the blog. Working with an agent with a hyper-local focus was important to them. The key to success in real estate is to commit to lead generation to catch buyers and sellers when you can.

Seek to catch buyers and sellers when you can!

DAY
23

SPINNING PLATES

In variety and acrobatic shows, often there is the spinning plate act. You have a visual already in your mind—of the performer using the gyroscopic effect and setting one plate spinning on a long pole. Then off to the next one and so on until the first spinning plate starts to wobble and requires attention.

This is a feat that many real estate agents attempt. It is that last spinning plate, though, that can cause all of them to come crashing down. The challenge is that there are so many opportunities, and some of them are good. The important consideration is if the activity is effective and if it is sustainable by the agent.

In the world of prospecting, options abound: hosting open houses; door knocking in a target neighborhood; connecting via social media, which has myriad choices; phone calls to both cold and warm leads; blogging; events; seminars; client parties; digital marketing; newsletters; handwritten notes; working with investors or flippers; purchasing leads from Internet sites; developing relationships with relocation companies; mass letter-writing campaigns; and pursuing expired or withdrawn seller listings. There are countless other options available—this list is not complete by any means.

Agents who build and grow a business focus on a few key strategies that go deep rather than wide. To keep with the analogy, it would look like successfully setting two plates in motion and sustaining the effort for at least one year. The benefit to this practice is that the agent can hold the activity accountable and determine whether it is actually an effective means of lead generation.

It is easy to find examples of agents who are successful at deep prospecting. An agent in our office focuses on the first-time homebuyer market by conducting seminars for people who currently live in apartment buildings. One agent works primarily with investors who buy and flip, and others who buy to hold and rent. Another agent has long-term relationships with relocation companies and has become an expert in that niche.

Now, each of these agents can confidently start another activity in motion. Only a very experienced, high-level performer would attempt to set two new plates spinning simultaneously. Agents would be wise to consider only one strategy at a time. Once it is set in motion and determined to be successful, then commence another one.

Set one new lead-generation activity successfully in motion prior to starting another one.

DAY 24

SECRETS OF LEAD GENERATION

My secret to success in lead generation can be summed up with these words: "The power of persistent, positive, professional, polite phoning and follow-through pays off!" This mantra is key for success as a real estate agent. Let's unpack these words by considering them in definition form.

Power is the ability to do something or to act in a particular way. Persistence is to firmly continue in a course of action in spite of difficulty or opposition. Positive is affirmative, or of constructive quality or attribute. Professional means a paid occupation rather than a hobby or pastime. Polite is to have or show behavior that is respectful and considerate of other people. Phoning is to give someone a call. Follow-through is the act of continuing a plan, project, scheme, or the like to its completion. Payoff is to receive money for services rendered.

The idea is to just do the "Ps" and not be tied to the outcome. The results, I have found, come from the consistency. It is like the "Energizer Bunny"—it keeps going and going and going. As inspiration, I keep one of the pink icons, complete with a drum, on my desk.

Agents ask me under what conditions I would consider not contacting someone. First, if the party is under a representation agreement with another broker, then it would be unethical to do so. And second, if they truly have asked me to stop. To quote the movie, *The Wolf of Wall Street,*

I stay in touch until the customer "buys or dies."

Commit to follow the "Ps" lead-generation practice today and the next day and so on.

DAY 25

ACRES OF LEADS

The classic story, *Acres of Diamonds*, is an ancient tale told by Russell Conwell that has been shared in countless motivational speeches. The story is of an African farmer who, not believing his own land was worth anything, sold it to travel the world in search of wealth. The farmer who acquired the land took the time to work with what he had. Although in a rough state at the time of purchase, he discovered through effort it held countless riches. Truly acres of diamonds were there the entire time.

In real estate, experience shows that successful agents work the market that they know best—most likely their neighborhood and surrounding community. To work with the people they know, their "sphere" in sales language. The market in which I live and practice real estate is high income and thus sales are at a higher dollar average than the surrounding communities. There are countless agents with offices in this market area, in order to capitalize on the potential. In effect, they drive past perfectly good opportunities in their own communities that they know well to search other marketplaces for wealth.

There is a real estate proverb that states an agent should list where he lives and sell to a buyer wherever he is licensed. The reason being is that listing a home for sale requires a deep knowledge of comparable properties, time is used more effectively servicing and showing a home that is close by, and owners have more confidence in an agent who has a vested interest in the sale. Selling a home to a buyer requires being able to, by license, open the door, negotiate the offer, and manage the logistics to settlement. This is also why most real estate agents new in the business begin by working with buyers.

The beauty of a tale such as this one is that it is timeless, in effect evergreen. The application stays true regardless of the market conditions.

The same is the case for many of the stories in this book. The stories are designed to stimulate and inspire you to take action. You have within you tremendous potential; start with what you have now. Connect to build and grow and you will discover the sweet spot of success in real estate.

Take action on the acres of leads that are around you and work them to their potential.

DAY
26

QUANTITY VERSUS QUALITY

Quantity versus quality is an age-old question. The debate is often heard in the platform regarding raising children. Which matters more, the amount of time spent with the child or the depth of interaction? Truly, I believe both are important. And it applies to the real estate profession as well, on several fronts.

In regard to experience, there is a school of thought that the number of years in the business is a good barometer to determine the quality of the agent. The best in real estate achieve that distinction by quantity of time. Other frequent standards of calculating success are based on number of transactions and the amount of dollar volume sold annually. And then, how many years the agent, team, and company have sustained those levels of achievement. The logic follows that whoever has the most business is the one who is the most qualified. Past performance is the best indicator of future success.

On the other side of the equation is the agent new in the business who does not have the quantity of experience in the industry to bring to the table. Yet many new agents succeed through their drive, hard work, and creativity. Unlike those who have been around a while, these agents often see new solutions and bring forth ideas that disturb the status quo in a positive way.

In lead generation, the quantity of activity can lead to quality. When a professional has an abundance of opportunity, the agent has more choices. Options include prioritizing the leads, referring out the business for a fee, and leveraging with other agents, team members, and staff. It often becomes a self-fulfilling prophecy that the more leads one has, the more leads one gets. The quality frequently increases with the quantity.

The client, too, has needs—both for quantity and quality time. Frequently customers ask how many listings an agent currently carries or how many buyers the agent is working with. The reason, I have discovered, for those questions is they feel deep down that at a certain number the agent won't have time to devote attention to them. And yet you have surely heard the Ben Franklin adage: "If you want something done, ask a busy person." With systems and standards of service, quality can be achieved with quantity.

Thus, we come full circle to the original statement. Both quantity and quality are necessary for a successful real estate agent.

Apply both quantity and quality principles to your clients, business, and life.

DAY

27

APP TRIES

It seems that new applications for my smartphone are available daily. How many times do you think the average user tries to use an application before deciding to stop? A survey of smartphone users has determined that it is 4.5.

The statistics for prospecting are similar. Salespeople stop trying to make contact after the fourth call in 90 percent of the cases. And yet 80 percent of sales are made after the fifth touch. The biggest impact you will make in your career as a real estate agent will be made after the majority of people have quit trying. That is powerful knowledge.

Think about how to apply smartphone strategies to real estate lead generation. First, you might reach out to others who have gone before to obtain recommendations on what to try to stay inspired. Next, reboot to get a "fresh screen," which could include going for a walk or meditating. Try another application and then return to the task, most likely with a fresh perspective. Do some research and then circle back; this time you might connect in a new way. And for the fifth try, just do it.

Just when you think you have your device or application figured out, something changes. There is an update to the software, which requires learning and adapting to the upgrade or perhaps even a completely new program. In prospecting, many agents give up too soon because of the fear of rejection. In either case, one direction is to fear the change and rejection and to either directly or passively resist taking any action.

The other, better way is to embrace the change and opportunity to connect as exciting and progressive. This perspective takes on the challenge to learn something new as forward-thinking and proactive. The same view applies to prospecting, as you consider how you can take the customer to the next level. No one really knows what the future holds. In a yogurt shop in Austin, there is a tip jar on the counter. It made me chuckle at the profound statement: "Fear change? Leave it here." Leave the fear behind and go enjoy your yogurt, learn a new app, or connect with a customer!

Dr. Orrison Swett Marden, inspirational author and founder of *Success* magazine, states: "There are two essential requirements for success. The first is "go-at-it-iveness" and the second is "stick-to-it-iveness." The professional real estate agent exhibits both!

Commit as much effort to lead generation as you would in learning a new smartphone application.

DAY
28

"YOU'VE GOT MAIL"

In the early years of the Internet, AOL was one of the primary providers of personal e-mail. The ding "You've got mail" as a notification became a trademark in American culture of the time. The romantic movie, *You've Got Mail*, capitalized on the times and the expectation of someone special wanting to connect.

In the ensuing years, e-mail has become one the most prevalent means of communication. Real estate agents at one time conducted business only in person or by document delivery services such as US mail and then FedEx. When fax machines became readily available, that mode of delivery increased the speed of communication. Now the majority of the transactional process of buying and selling a home is conducted by e-mail or some form of digital delivery. Due to the volume of e-mail most people receive, it has lost the personal element for many.

The proactive, customer-service-oriented agent provides consistent professional communication to clients. Sellers love to hear feedback about their homes. Buyers want to know about what houses are available that meet their criteria. There exists for the professional real estate agent the happy expectation of someone wanting to connect. Rather than using an auto-delivery feedback service for sellers, share tidbits and more personal antidotes from open house and agent feedback. With buyers, instead of using auto-alert services for new listings, take the time to personally view the homes. Then deliver the information that is above and beyond what the buyer will learn off the Internet listing. These are e-mails that customers and clients are sure to read and connect with.

All agents prefer that there only be positive communication to share with clients. Sadly there are occasions when people void the contract, the home inspection indicates serious issues with the property, and agents share negative feedback about an owner's home. In these instances, experience shows that it is best to share the information via phone or in person. A follow-up e-mail that provides an overview of the conversation and options and action items is appropriate, though. In that way, the agent maintains a high level of professionalism in communication, while at the same time recognizes that certain situations and client personal preferences warrant different styles.

There are some clients who prefer other means of communication, such as texting. Again, keep in mind that the transaction and relationship is professional and that strong written documentation of all communication is part of an agent's best practices protocol.

Utilize the positive expectation of "you've got mail" to communicate with customers and clients.

THROW SPAGHETTI AGAINST THE WALL TO SEE WHAT STICKS

Experienced pasta cooks have a saying: "Throw the spaghetti against the wall and see what sticks." The reason being, if the pasta sticks, then you know it is cooked. Another interpretation is that it isn't possible to know what will stick, in most cases, until we actually do it. Trying to figure that out by sitting back and waiting to see what sticks doesn't provide any more information.

This saying is one my deceased business partner, Sue Huckaby, would frequently proclaim with her charming southern accent. Listing agents prepare a comparative market analysis (CMA) for seller clients. The CMA is the industry standard to understand the current market conditions and to assist the seller in establishing a market list price. Until the home actually goes on the active market, though, there is no way to truly know the outcome. Once the property is on the market, in effect the market is the market study. The level of activity and feedback are strong indicators of whether the list price was "cooked" thoroughly enough, to use the pasta analogy.

Author Amy Wilkinson, in the book *The Creator's Code: 6 Essential Skills of Extraordinary Entrepreneurs*, references a study performed with two groups of people with the objective to create a project. One group of participants was provided with as many supplies as they needed and were encouraged to try multiple times to create the project. The other group was only given the supplies for one project and told that they were to think and plan before they built the "perfect" project. The successful group was the one that had the opportunity to try and fail, because they learned so much each time they tried it. It was in the actual doing that the best outcome was achieved.

Real estate is an active pursuit. It is in the engagement with the market and clients in real time that determines what pricing strategy works—and thus sticks. This phenomenon applies to lead generation, as well. The agent who proactively prospects consistently on a daily basis is like the experimental group that was encouraged to try multiple times. Real estate is not a "one-and-done" endeavor.

Throwing spaghetti against the wall is the best way to know whether it is fully cooked; putting a home on the market is the best way to know how the market will respond. And consistent business development is the best way to achieve and sustain success as a real estate agent.

Take action to achieve best results in market knowledge and business development.

DAY 30

TAKE THE NEXT STEP

Inquiring agents often want to know how often to contact prospects. On the continuum of doing nothing to being considered a pushy salesperson, there are a lot of choices in between. One of the secrets to my success is that I had the attitude of being helpful to people. And so I would just take the next natural step.

An example of a situation that happens frequently is someone stops me in the grocery store, at church, or at book club and asks me about the home down the street that is on the market or recently sold. We chat briefly and then I tell them I will do some research and get back to them. This enables me to get their contact information if I don't have it already. If it is about a particular home and I haven't seen it yet, then I will go see the home. Afterwards I call or send a follow-up e-mail with the requested information. My goal is to do so within twenty-four hours, no later than forty-eight hours. On occasion, I also send a handwritten note thanking them for reaching out to me and to let them know I am always available to assist with any of their real estate needs or questions.

Many agents naturally do this. What happens next is what I believe makes the difference, and that is to keep the conversation going. Enter the person's contact information in your database. This step helps you build your database to grow your business. Then put a "watch" on the house they inquired about or set up an alert to follow up with them. With some gentle probing, I ask if they are in the market to buy or sell a home. At this juncture, people are typically forthcoming and I have a better sense of next steps. Then I just "put them in the pipeline" to stay in touch.

How often I contact them from that point forward depends on several factors. Of course, I will contact them when they ask me to, usually just a bit ahead of schedule. If they get in touch with me in the meantime, I mirror their step, again usually just one step ahead but not pushy. It is like dancing the tango: move with confidence and try not to step on anyone's feet. If there is new or relevant information, I send that. Typically I reach out a minimum of one or two times per year just to stay in touch, to see if anything has changed, and to offer my assistance. This contact is a gentle reminder that I am an active real estate agent and want to earn their business.

What I see that challenges agents is just taking the next step. The words of Antoine de Saint-Exupery are my inspiration: "What saves a man is to take a step. Then another step. It is always the same step, but you have to take it." Really, the step I have found doesn't matter nearly as much as the action of actually taking it.

The quote applies equally well to building and growing a business. To paraphrase: "What builds and grows a business is to take a step. Then another step. It is always the same step, but you have to take it."

Take the next step today!

DAY
31

VIRTUOUS CYCLE

The concept of a virtuous cycle has applications in economics and management theory. It is based on the idea that success leads to more success via the feedback loop. The reverse concept is that of the vicious cycle, when circumstances spiral in a negative and undesirable direction.

An example that comes to mind is that of weight training. In the beginning, the results of the exercise are not obvious. The athlete completes the movements based on the knowledge of the future benefit promised. At some point, the exerciser feels stronger and has more energy, sees the toning of the muscles, and recognizes the health benefits of increased metabolism. As results become more apparent, the virtuous cycle causes the exerciser to commit and remain consistent in the program.

In real estate, those new to the profession have to trust in the process, as it takes time to build the virtuous cycle. The sales cycle in real estate is much longer than in many industries. One simple way to create a virtuous cycle is by staying in touch with and cultivating past client relationships. Homeowners move, on average, once every seven years, which in many cases can mean both a buy and a sell transaction. Further, many salespeople build their business on referrals, which are frequently obtained from happy past clients. Providing quality service to referrals is also a positive self-fulfilling prophecy. People want to refer business to people who provide top-notch professional service.

Listings are another opportunity to create positive momentum in a real estate business. With a listing, an agent has the opportunity to conduct marketing that goes beyond the sale of just the one home. Agents, in many cases, meet other sellers while hosting public open houses and neighbor receptions, by door knocking, or calling those living in the neighborhood. Those sellers may be in the market soon to sell their home. Buyers often contact listing agents directly for information about the home for sale, which opens up a dialogue that can potentially turn into a client relationship. Mailing just-listed and just-sold postcards to homes surrounding the listing or buyer-represented sale are also known to generate additional opportunities. Statistically, for every listing sold, professional agents on average generate one additional buyer or seller lead.

There is also the mental virtuous cycle. When one is on a positive roll, the chain of events feed themselves in a favorable direction. In the words of Warren Buffett: "Time is the friend of the wonderful habits, the enemy of the mediocre ones."

Professional agents consistently take those actions that continue this success-oriented momentum.

Establish and sustain activities that project your business and life into a virtuous cycle.

MEET CUTE

A "meet cute" occurs when a couple meets for the first time. Most common in romantic comedies in movies or on television, it sets the stage for a future relationship. The scene unfolds with them meeting in either an embarrassing circumstance or a humorous clash of personalities or situation.

As a real estate agent, I have experienced "meet cute" situations with future clients. One such occasion was on a flight to Texas to visit family for the Christmas holiday. As many people do, I struck up a conversation with the gentleman sitting next to me. I asked if he was going home, or if he lived in the DC metro area. He explained that he was heading to San Diego to visit family and that he lived in Falls Church, Virginia. As we had just purchased an investment town home in Falls Church, I delved deeper into the closest intersection. It turned out that he lived on the next street over from our property and went on to share that he was renting.

A "meet cute" opportunity just landed in my lap. After explaining that I was a real estate agent, he indicated that he wanted to purchase a home after the New Year. Contact information was exchanged and future plans were made to see houses when he returned from the holiday.

Other people can have a "meet cute" and when they think of you as a real estate agent it can turn into an opportunity. An occasion that comes to mind involves my husband. He sits on the board of an organization and during a coffee break conversation with a fellow board member, it came up that I was a real estate agent. Turned out that his daughter was pregnant with her second child and the couple was looking to move into a single-family home so that they could have a yard. Andy put me in touch and that led to both selling the young couple a home, and also listing and selling their town home.

The secret, I believe, for "meet cute" opportunities is to be open to the possibility. Truly, any situation has the potential. And share with those you know that you are open to their "meet cute" scenarios as well!

Look for "meet cute" lead-generation opportunities in your life!

AUTOPILOT

The takeoff and landing of a plane are key moments that require a pilot's full attention. Once in the air at cruising altitude, though, the autopilot performs a vital function. With autopilot, the plane will fly on course, thereby reducing the pilot's workload and fatigue. The autopilot takes care of the basic functions of speed, maintaining altitude, and staying on course so that the pilot can focus his attention on those situations that require a thinking person. Systems are to a real estate agent what autopilot is for a pilot.

First, agents should establish a system for prospecting. This can be set up as activity blocking, which means to contact a set number of people each working day, or time blocking, which is a set amount of time per day allocated to that task. Once this process is set up in place and functions smoothly, the professional agent can put it on autopilot.

The next system to establish is one that tracks leads and sets up a plan for follow-through. This often occurs simultaneously with lead-generation activities. Some agents use a database such as Wise Agent, Top Producer, or Contractually. Keep in mind that some of these tasks can be performed by a staff person, which is both an autopilot and leverage strategy. Once the systems are in place, then everyone knows their responsibilities and can be held accountable to metrics daily.

Advertising, distribution of postcards or mailers, social media, and other content-related marketing activities, once in place, can be put on autopilot with monitoring. Our team has staff members who oversee all of these functions under agent direction. In the beginning, as is typical of a new real estate agent, I did all of this. As the business grew, staff took on more and more of these types of responsibilities.

My husband is a private pilot and reminds me that it is during takeoff and landing when the pilot needs to pay the most attention. So it is with a real estate practice, as well; when getting the systems off the ground, the agent should plan to put in the most effort and time.

There can be a danger to autopilot that I must warn you about. Flying a plane is still a hands-on operation; it requires a thinking person. Sometimes putting a system on autopilot causes one to become complacent, and then fail to check in and verify that everything is operating properly and as intended. Autopilot can be your ally when everything is running smoothly, and your enemy if it gets off course or isn't sufficiently monitored. The key to this success strategy is to remain always vigilant.

Determine what systems can be put on autopilot so that you can focus on the more demanding opportunities of the business.

DAY 34

SHORT-TERM PAIN—LONG-TERM GAIN

When something is challenging, especially in the beginning, it is tempting to quit before the results can be felt. An example of this, for me, is weight training. At the start of my program, all I felt was sore! Yet, it is after sustained effort that one starts to reap the benefits. Seth Godin, in *The Dip*, has a great litmus test to use when in doubt: "Never quit something with great long-term potential just because you can't deal with the stress of the moment."

For success as a real estate agent, the sustained effort of effective business development has the greatest long-term potential. Even when top agents don't feel like it, the professionals generate leads day after day.

How does one power through the pain or stress of the moment? There are many proven success strategies. One is to set an appointment on the calendar to prospect, just like I do for my personal training sessions. Another is to work with an accountability partner. If someone is expecting you to be there, you will more likely keep the commitment. Track your progress; being able to see how far you have come is empowering. Create consequences for unmet expectations. For example, work an additional four hours on the weekend if lead-generation goals have not been achieved during the workweek. On the positive side, establish rewards, big and small, for reached milestones.

As way of example, this is personal story of how consequence and reward led to completion of a very important goal. In high school, our son was very close to achieving the rank of Eagle Scout. All that was left was his project. Becoming an Eagle Scout is an accomplishment that his father and I knew, later in life, he would be very glad that he completed. At the time, all he could see was that he had other things he wanted to pursue.

The Boy Scouts call it the siren call of "grades, gas, and girls" that lures young men away. At the time, Drew was very close to being of age to obtain his driver's license. So his father and I created the combined consequence-reward scenario that we would take him to obtain his license "once the Eagle had landed." Until it was done, our assistance was not available. You never did see such a motivated young man; it was truly amazing the speed at which the project was completed.

Remember, no one is making you be a real estate agent. You chose this as a profession, so you can choose to be successful at it.

The short-term pain of prospecting may be difficult, yet it is worth the long-term gain of a successful business.

DAY
35

"DANCE LIKE NOBODY'S WATCHING"

Agents new to the real estate profession often feel that customers may not want to work with them because they are newly licensed and thus don't have experience. Established agents can get stuck in ineffective processes and find that change needs to happen in order to take their business to the next level. It is true for both that the only way that one obtains experience is by actually getting out there and doing it. It is a catch-22. At the beginning of any endeavor, everyone starts out at the same place, with no experience.

In the popular song by Austin & Ally, "Dance Like Nobody's Watching," these lines resonate: "What will they think, you're so afraid to make a move; you're second-guessing every, every step." The answer in the song is to dance anyway. The answer to the new real estate agent is to take a chance anyway. Contact friends, relatives, associates, and neighbors anyway. The answer to the seasoned agent is to make the changes anyway, even though you don't have firm assurance it will work.

Yes, some may be "naysayers." Yet some new ideas may work. The only way to show the world that you can do it is by doing it. Sing the words for inspiration if you need to: "Forget about what everyone else says, show 'em what you got and that you're ready to rock it."

It may seem safe to only work with people who don't know you are a new agent, and to stay in the comfort zone of hosting open houses and prospecting among people whom you don't know well. Those are proven methods of getting a new agent's business off the ground, to be sure. At some point, though, you have to stop second-guessing every step.

For the experienced agent, to build and grow a business frequently requires advancing to a new level or market. That means operating outside one's comfort zone, into the growth zone. New and longtime agents both benefit from dancing anyway. At first it may appear no one is watching. Once you achieve and sustain success in real estate, though, you will show them what you've got.

Dance from your comfort zone into an arena of growth.

DAY

36

LICENSED TO VIEW HOUSES

In the James Bond *007* movie, the secret agent is authorized per the title: "Licensed to kill." Real estate agents are "licensed to view houses" and should be anything but secret agents if they want to be successful.

In order to sell houses in the US, real estate agents must be licensed by the jurisdiction in which they want to conduct business. The purpose for issuing and governing the licensure is to protect the consumer. This is a worthy objective, given that the transaction of buying and selling a home is most people's largest financial purchase, ongoing obligation, and sale. Further, the licensure assures for the seller the security and safety of the property as a responsibility of those who are allowed access.

Real estate agents frequently take for granted that this is an additional benefit of licensure—having the right of access to people's homes that are on the market for sale. There are some occasions when the public is permitted to view, but in most cases that is at open-house events. The agent, though, is presented with substantially more ingress. Sometimes access is granted via lock box, either secure or combination. Sometimes that access is granted at special Realtors® events, such as broker open houses. Sometimes access is granted via the listing agent with appointment-only homes and properties.

Knowledge of the inventory is one of the best ways for real estate agents to become experts in their markets. Being permitted to view houses is one of the benefits of being licensed that differentiates a real estate agent from the general public. All professional agents should take full advantage of this right!

Keeping current on the inventory is the best way to generate leads and be a true neighborhood expert.

DAY
37

LEVERAGE WITH MEDIA

Agents can become known experts on their local markets by writing blogs and articles for publications and social media outlets. Barbara Corcoran, star of ABC's *Shark Tank*, made her fortune selling residential real estate. She put her name on the map in New York City, though, by writing a market report she named *The Corcoran Report*.

I incorporated Barbara's idea and expanded it into my marketplace a number of years ago by writing a quarterly market report. In addition, agents on our team write and submit "Where we live," personal-interest stories about neighborhoods and community events. The local media is delighted to have great content to publish, and in almost all cases the article is printed word-for-word. Agents become known as true "local neighborhood experts" via social media, as well. Everyone loves to read about what is going on in their community and what makes it special.

This is effectively free public relations and influences the public significantly more than paid advertising. Some experts place the value of a third-party endorsement at twenty times that of traditional branding efforts and advertising. The media publication can also become a tool for lead generation. Agents use their neighborhood interest story to door knock and meet the community face-to-face. It makes for a "warm call" to have the story as the introductory piece.

The market report is a valuable tool at listing appointments, as well. Sellers are quite impressed when they see that the local paper considers the report relevant for publication. A case in point is friends from church, who called me in November to set up a time to visit about listing their home. They were going to wait until the spring, yet after reading my market report in the paper, decided that it was a good time to sell.

Social media offers multiple platforms available to the agent for connection and promotion. The most popular portals are in a state of constant change and evolution. Keys to success include staying abreast of current trends and being relevant. Synergy with other media is a great approach for a comprehensive media plan. To be effective, the best in the business find a niche and are in constant dialogue with their constituencies. Author and mega agent Tony Giordano in "the social agent" states the opportunity best: "We have been given the ability to network in ways never dreamed of - and anywhere in the world."

Leveraging media is a powerful force, as there is the potential for exponential exposure. It is one of the foundational strategies of success for the professional real estate agent. In the words of PT Barnum: "Without promotion, something terrible happens . . . nothing!" Make sure something happens in your real estate business!

Leverage media to promote awareness of your brand.

DAY
38

ARE YOU MY PRIORITY?

To be a successful, real estate agents require the ability to prioritize. This is when many people get stumped: "What is a priority?" Is it keeping a deal together by managing the contract to the settlement part of the transaction? Is it attending a training event to learn about social media? Is it going to lunch with a vendor? The question reminds me of the baby bird in the Dr. Seuss classic, *Are You My Mother?* The bird is in pursuit of her mother and in the meantime is distracted by many look-alikes and potential mother substitutes.

Barbara Corcoran, who made her fortune building and selling a real estate empire, The Corcoran Group, is now known as one of the full-time investors on the reality show, *Shark Tank*. One of her key questions to the entrepreneurs before she invests in them is: "Where has your business come from so far?"

According to Barbara, unfortunately it seems most don't know. So do you know? Her fundamental rule is to first determine the source of your business. Figure out what works and what doesn't. Then you can focus your time and resources on those priorities. Pursue tried-and-true methods prior to embarking on any new ventures.

I discovered the truth of this principle a few years into my career. My most successful lead-generation activity had been mailing "just sold" postcards to my sphere. As my business focus moved from working primarily with buyers to listing homes, I decided to invest instead in glossy print advertising. The resources were not there to do both, so I stopped sending the postcards. The impact of my decision became apparent within a few months. The leads from my primary client base, my sphere, had all but dried up. It took a few months to turn the ship around and undo the damage, yet it was a strong lesson learned. Now my first priority is to know where my business comes from and keep my focus there.

The answer to the questions above lies in saying "no" to everything that isn't directly related to income-producing activities. As Barbara goes on to say: "I don't let them spend any time on anything that doesn't directly result in a sale. Because that's what you need when you're a small business." Thus, if the management of the contract can be handled by other parties, then it isn't the priority for the day. If social media is your primary source of prospecting, then attending training to improve is a key aspect to business development. If the vendor has provided leads to you in the past, then it is definitely a good use of your time to have lunch with him. That's how I answer the question daily: "Are you my priority?"

Focus first on income-producing activities
that lead directly to business.

DAY
39

YOU CAN START AT ANY TIME

The day most people start a new habit or activity is New Year's Day. The calendar change promises a new beginning. Studies show only 8 percent of people actually achieve the resolutions established then. The secret is that you can start at any time by thinking success and then doing those activities on a daily basis to build a sustainable habit. That is how I have achieved my success vision and you can, too, by starting today.

I became a licensed real estate agent in July 2002. My broker at the time encouraged me to contact people on a daily basis to tell them I was now selling real estate. Nothing unusual about that process—it's what most brokers tell new agents.

The difference is that I created a means of personal accountability to keep track of how many people I contacted every day. I used a very low-tech, spiral-bound notebook that conveniently had twenty-five lines on each page. Every Monday I numbered a new page from one to twenty-five. I knew exactly where I was in completing the work I set out for myself each week.

I still have that notebook from my first year in the business and show it to new agents as evidence that I really did what I recommend that they do. Out of the twenty-five of that first week in the business, I converted three leads into actual transactions that year. The stories are a testimony to how a commitment to daily prospecting can lead to success.

One of the contacts I made was a friend who was going through a divorce. I sold her a small home for herself and her children. She remarried a few years later, and I sold that house and sold them a much larger newer home. A number of years later, her husband sold his company and they upgraded to an upper-bracket home and our team sold their current property. With that one lead, my team sold more than $6 million in real estate.

Another couple I met that week also stands out because of the multiple transactions through the years—six in total, plus one referral. I met them via a sign call, not the easiest lead-conversion opportunity, particularly for a new agent. As newlyweds, they were ready to buy their first condo. When she became pregnant a couple years later, as often happens they needed more space so moved up to a town home. And of course I sold the condo. Well, I'm sure you can imagine the rest of the story. As his career progressed and they had more income, each child then translated into a larger home, which meant selling their smaller abode. That one lead has resulted in almost $4 million in transactions. The secret I found is to track the business source and stay in touch with past clients. Both are keys to success in building and growing a business.

This proves that you can start at any time. It was the middle of August, nothing particularly special about that week other than I decided to begin.

Commit today to lead generation and track the sources of business.

WHO YOU GONNA CALL?

"Who you gonna call?" is a line from the lyrics of the 1980's movie *Ghostbusters*. It has one of those crazy tunes that can get stuck in my head. The application to real estate is that by the creation of brand awareness, when people have a real estate need or referral, they will think of you. It should come as no surprise that if people do not know you are a real estate agent, they aren't going to call. This is a key objective to real estate success, to not be a secret agent.

It often is the case that most people know several real estate agents. This is true for other professions, as well. For example, we are friends with several CPAs, insurance agents, financial advisors, attorneys, restaurant owners, car dealers, and numerous other service providers and professionals. Marketing gurus have metrics on how to create top-of-mind awareness. It is a key component to build and grow a business that sustains long-term success.

There is a part of the brain known as the reticular activating system (RAS). It is the portal through which nearly all information enters the brain. It serves as a filter for incoming data and affects what a person focuses on and thus remembers. People are bombarded constantly with messages, so the RAS is like a bouncer that determines what is important and what should be stored away. It files away what may be useful later on. This is when being top-of-mind as a real estate agent becomes important. The idea is that when people have a real estate need or question or knows someone who does, they will think of you as an agent who can meet that need.

An example of the phenomenon is when people begin the process of buying a new car. All of a sudden, it seems they see the cars they are considering everywhere. They start to pay attention to advertising and media and are pleasantly surprised when in conversation that other people also have information and interest in the car purchase. This is the RAS at work. The marketing presence more than likely was always there, they just didn't notice it. To achieve success as a real estate professional requires being relevant all the time to the public. Then when the occasion arises, the customer will think of you. An inconsistent message is not as effective.

There are countless marketing, advertising, social media, promotional, public relations, and lead-generation platforms for creating top-of-mind brand awareness. The important message to the agent is to do something and to do it on a consistent basis in order to build and grow a successful business.

Establish top-of-mind awareness platforms on a consistent basis for strong name identification in the marketplace.

DAY 41

TRACK YOUR WAY TO SUCCESS

In the movie *The Martian*, the main character, played by Matt Damon, is left behind on Mars. The circumstances in the story were the antagonist, as there were limited resources. This made survival virtually impossible. When he realized the gravity of the situation, he began a video journal as both a chronicle and a means of thinking his way to solutions.

Keeping a log or journal is a time-tested way to discover what is and isn't working. To think about and reflect on collected information often reveals solutions not previously considered. Adjustments can then be made and further evaluations provide even more enterprising solutions.

In the beginning of my real estate career, I kept a log of all the people I talked to about real estate. At first, this was primarily a means of personal accountability. In order to keep a record of all of the information I gathered, I moved it into a database. After I touch someone, I input any updates into the database. It makes for a much richer follow-through when you actually remember everything you talked about the last time you connected. The database also allows me to better track key metrics, such as the source of leads and when next to follow up with customers.

To take my business to the next level, I began to work with a business coach. She encouraged me to keep a journal—five minutes a day of reflection. When first recommended, I am embarrassed to admit

I proclaimed I did not have five minutes a day to spare.

Then I considered the fact that I was paying her to help me break through mindset and practices that were keeping me from achieving a higher level of success. So I told her I would "try" it. For more than one year, I have written one page per day in a journal. The amazing thing is that great truths have been revealed in the process. It has helped me make changes in my business and life that I want and need to do.

High-producing agent, podcast host, and author Pat Hiban, in *6 Steps to 7 Figures*, shows a photo of all the journals he has kept in his career. Clearly it demonstrates that success leaves clues. Solutions are clearer and new ideas are revealed—no need to be stranded on Mars to track and journal your way to success in real estate here on earth.

Keep a log or journal to track and reflect on solutions to take your business and life to the next level.

DAY
42

JUST KEEP SWIMMING

People with young kids in their lives will recognize "just keep swimming" from Dory's song in *Finding Nemo*.

If I were to write a letter of advice to myself as a newly licensed real estate agent, Dory's wise words would be at the top of my list. The area in which agents need to "just keep swimming" the most is in prospecting. If you are a swimmer, remember when you first learned? To perform the strokes correctly felt awkward and were difficult at first. And yet over time, as you perfected a stroke, you began to feel the power of moving through the water with speed and ease. That is the way it is with lead generation. Commit to learn the strokes of business development and over time strength and skill will build and grow so that you will flow through the process with ease.

Another lesson from "just keep swimming" is to stay on task. To constantly switch up strokes can cause a swimmer to lose momentum. Professional athletes concentrate on the perfection of one or two strokes to achieve the best results. Real estate professionals should hone one or two lead-generation methods before pursuing the mastery of others. Concentration of effort makes for a much stronger and more impactful connection than a scattered effect does.

It can be beneficial to have a new agent observe and shadow a more seasoned professional. Training and role-playing are valuable also. But at some point, the agent has to get in the water. Standing on the side of the pool is the metaphor for the agent who spends all of his time in training, thus attempting to learn to swim by sitting on the sidelines. Nothing replaces jumping in the water. The learning is in the doing and then you "just keep swimming."

Barbara Corcoran, in her book *Shark Tales*, shares the story of how she landed on the show *Shark Tank*. She was selected in the initial round to be one of the "sharks," but then at the last minute discovered she was cut for someone younger. Rather than getting discouraged and quitting, she sent an e-mail message to the producer with the subject line: "still swimming." Even when there are sharks in the water and the barracuda attacks, the professional "just keeps swimming."

"Just keep swimming" in lead generation to maintain persistence in developing and growing a business.

ACTION TRACTION

Newton's first law states that an object at rest stays at rest, and an object in motion stays in motion. One of the distinctions between those who just barely make it in real estate and those who are successful is related to this fundamental law. In effect, an agent at rest stays at rest and an agent in motion stays in motion. By getting into motion and taking action, the agent gains traction that then gains forward momentum.

This is particularly true in the case of lead generation. Consistent, active prospecting becomes a self-fulfilling prophesy. If an agent is in a slump, there are a number of things that she can do to get productive. They all involve action.

One is to go see houses. Many agents become Realtors® because they love houses. So viewing homes should be a positive activity for the agent. While looking at houses, the agent should think about people they who know might be interested. If they know anyone who lives in the neighborhood or community, this is a great chance to connect, as well.

Door knocking is another lead-generation method that immediately gets agents into productive activity. One of the agents on our team recently door knocked in her mother's neighborhood. Nothing immediately came of it, but within weeks one of the neighbors was ready to put his home on the market. He thought of this agent because of the flyer she left at the home. He wanted to hire a proactive agent who didn't just sit around waiting for the business to come to her.

Community events, charity fundraisers, children's school functions, and sporting outings are all opportunities for the agent to meet and network with people. Even when you don't feel like getting out, just doing so is a positive motion. The words of self-improvement author and speaker Dale Carnegie attest to this: "Inaction breeds doubt and fear. Action breeds confidence and courage. If you want to conquer fear, do not sit at home and think about it. Go out and get busy." Gain some traction to your action!

Get into action today and stay in action to support your lead-generation objectives.

DAY
44

EVERYBODY KNOWS SOMEBODY

There are over two million licensed real estate agents in the United States. It goes without saying that most people will know several real estate professionals, some of whom might be a friend, relative, associate, or neighbor. The situation presents over and over that some people select me as their agent and others don't. People have very valid reasons for the choice they make.

One of the key reasons people select an agent other than one they know is because of concern that being in a business transaction will possibly damage the friendship. This is an opportunity for the agent to take the high road. If doing business together becomes a problem, it is contractually based and not a true friendship. This is the perspective I share with people when this objection comes up. My friendship with them is the priority and I want them to do what is best for their situation.

The other concern people voice is that if a difficult situation were to arise during the transaction, they wouldn't want to have to "fire" or have to confront someone they know. This more often happens with sellers, and typically involves the pricing and marketing of the home. The best response to this situation is to keep the communication on a professional level at all times. Establish the protocol to follow standards of service and procedures uniformly with all customers and clients. This is important even if the client is a friend and seems to prefer a more casual approach. In this manner, the client recognizes that you as the agent treat transactions as business, not personally. This conveys the assurance by your actions and demeanor that you are "on the job," watching out for their interests.

The strongest reason buyers and sellers give for selecting an agent they know to represent them is that they want someone who cares about them at a personal level. As the home is most people's largest financial transaction and the buying and selling of it can be emotional, many find it to be helpful to have a friend on their side. Agents have the fiduciary and ethical responsibility to provide a high degree of service to all clients. From my personal experience, when I work with people I know, I put in that extra effort and energy because I am additionally motivated by the relationship. There is a stronger mutual interest that goes beyond the monetary aspects to the transaction. It is very important to me that my friends be happy with their decision and our continuing friendship.

Another scenario is what happens if they know several agents; how do they decide who to hire? When I am presented with this question I recommend selection based on performance criteria, as past results often are the best indicator of future outcomes. Everybody knows somebody—use these scripts and dialogues to achieve great success!

Practice your response for when people you know bring up the concern of whether or not they should work with a friend.

DAY
45

ARE YOU A QUARTERBACK OR RECEIVER?

In high school, my husband played football. I didn't know him then, but have heard many stories. During the fall season with football in the air, I of course think of real estate applications.

In football, the quarterback (QB) is the one who directs the offensive play of the team. As the leader, the quarterback has the option to play the ball himself by running, to hand the ball off, or throw the ball to a teammate downfield. The QB position is the most visual and well-known.

In real estate, the quarterback is the lead generator or sometimes known as the rainmaker. The agent who generates the leads has control of the situation. In football, the eye is on the ball. In real estate, the eye is on the lead. As the lead generator, the agent can decide to run with the lead himself. Or the agent can refer the lead to a teammate or other agent.

The receiver is a valuable player too, often the fastest on the football team. In most cases, it is the receiver who does the happy dance in the end zone after a touchdown. The receiver combines the skills of running and outmaneuvering the defensive players, all the while keeping his eye on the ball in order to make a connection. In some cases, the receiver plays a defensive role, as in the case of an interception.

The referral agent in the real estate industry is also a key player. Passing the lead can be a strong strategy in the building of a real estate team.

A professional agent who can convert the lead to settlement is equal to the player who makes the touchdown. Everyone on the team wins.

Play the best position in your business and life!

DAY

46

THE PEPSI™ CHALLENGE

Most people know several real estate agents. This frequently comes up in conversations I have when people find out that I am in the profession. Typically they tell me about the other agents they know or have worked with in the past. Whether I know the agents they are speaking about or not, I stay positive and am careful not to disparage colleagues. Either way, I share that there are more than a thousand agents in our immediate market area, over 154,000 in the international brokerage with which I am affiliated with and two million active real estate licenses in the United States. Most people are surprised at the number of people in the industry.

It is important to view this dialogue as an open door to offer your services. If people are adamant that they already have an agent, I offer my services if anything ever changes. Many times agents retire or leave the profession. Another common scenario is the agent who helped them buy the house isn't strong as a listing agent. So when people go to sell, they very likely will be looking for an agent who has those skills or a more in-depth marketing platform. To bring in a bit of humor, I share that it can be like the "Pepsi™ challenge": in numerous blind taste tests, people select Pepsi™ over Coke™. Maybe that will be the case for them.

Another script that I have had success with is the offer of a "second opinion." If they or someone close to them were considering surgery or a significant medical procedure, wouldn't they likely interview more than one doctor? Given that the sale of a home is likely their largest financial transaction, wouldn't they be interested in having more than one agent make a presentation?

A response that people will sometimes make is that they don't want to waste my time. This is when I emphasize that it is my job to work with sellers to help them in the marketing and sale of their home. It is not an inconvenience to show buyers houses, as that is an opportunity for me to observe in person how I can help them achieve their wants and needs. Neither of these activities are ever a waste of my time. These are some of the key functions of my job as a real estate agent.

Getting into an active relationship with the customer also creates a reciprocity loop. It is in the giving of time and services that customers are more likely to want to give back, as well. Once they see how eager you are to help them, it can open the door to a client relationship.

Employ effective dialogues on the services you provide as a real estate agent, particularly when competing for the business.

DAY

47

PREVIEW HOMES AS MUSE!

I love to visit with new agents to hear their stories about why they chose the residential real estate profession. The reasons many share are that they love houses and people and thought it would be a great combination. That is the essence of my story, as well. And yet it surprises me how many agents don't actually go see houses on a regular basis now that they are free to do so at practically any time.

In most market areas, there is a day set aside for broker tours of listings. Typically these opens are for homes new to the market. So it is a great opportunity for agents to stay fresh on the inventory. Also, homes that are appointment-only often can be more challenging to view, thus the broker open tour is the best chance to see the home. I do my best to set aside this day to see as many homes as I can, as well as to network with other real estate agents.

Einstein believed that "combinatory play" was a central feature in his creative thinking process. By putting your focus on something you find enjoyable, it can release the stress from trying to force a solution. I'm sure you've had this happen to you as well. Einstein played the violin. Others practice yoga, paint, go for a walk, or listen to music as their source of inspiration. And then the answer comes like a flash of brilliance.

Previewing homes can be a great business development opportunity. For one, the action itself gets the agent out of the office and into the field. For agents with a true passion for homes, going to see houses is a form of play. The change of scenery is a winning strategy for me when I am stuck in a rut or in a funk.

It is important to not take your muse for granted. I'm sure you have heard of writer's block, which occurs when the flow of ideas has stopped. The same effect can happen to real estate professionals. In Ray Bradbury's book, *Zen in the Art of Writing: Releasing the Creative Genius within You*, the author speaks of the importance of the care and feeding of one's muse. In this way, the subconscious then goes to work on an idea or inspiration.

Previewing homes is a way to care for and feed your muse! When I preview homes I think of people. By being out in the marketplace, inspiration of potential sellers and buyers to touch base with comes to me. New information to follow through on is more evident when the agent is out in the actual marketplace. Take care of your muse and it will take care of you!

Play at viewing houses as a source of inspiration for business development.

DAY
48

THERE IS NO "TRY"

Sellers often will say that they want to try and sell their home. Another version of this sentiment is to test the market. The implication is that they will only sell if they can achieve the price that they want. This is truly a situation of not being a "real seller."

The wisdom of Yoda in the *Star Wars* movies comes to mind: "Do or do not: there is no try!" Something happens when a person makes a decision to *do*. At that crossroads, she believes that it will happen and takes the steps necessary to make it occur. For a true seller, this includes preparing the home for show condition and pricing it such that it is "in the market" with comparable properties.

The trouble with just "trying" is that it implies one foot is in the "do it" camp and one foot is on the "don't do it" side. I have found that this, in effect, sends mixed messages to the market. Buyers pick up quickly the behavior of a real seller, and vice versa. The seller may be "on the market" but not "in the market," which is best defined as the range that sends the message that she is ready, willing, and able to sell.

The same principle can hold true with real estate agents. Those who "try" real estate often have a backup plan: if real estate doesn't work out, she will just go back to teaching or pharmaceutical sales or whatever was the agent's previous profession. Another scenario that often occurs if a person isn't successful as a real estate agent is that she will look to related fields, such as with a lender, property management firm, or settlement company.

Lead generation is an activity I have found that agents often "try" more than they "do." They will "try" knocking on doors, yet when nothing happens after the first ten houses, they give up. Or they will "try" open houses and yet not follow through completely with the visitors. Or they will "try" sending out postcards, yet only do it one or two times and then discontinue because it didn't work.

The challenge with all of these scenarios is that full effort was not expended. It takes considerably more than "trying" to be successful as a real estate agent. It takes a lot of "doing."

Take Yoda's words to heart and just "do."

RIDE UPHILL FIRST

Cycling outdoors is one of my favorite activities. When my husband and I map out a ride, we always strive to do the hardest segment first. This typically means riding uphill. The benefit of following this plan is that once we reach the half-way mark, it almost always means that the second half is predominately downhill. On long rides, we reward ourselves for doing the difficult work first by stopping for lunch or a cup of coffee and small treat. This is smart from an energy standpoint, as well, as clearly we are strongest at the start of the ride and fatigue sets in as we rack up the miles.

The reason why many coaches recommend that real estate agents commit to lead generation in the morning is based on the same principle as riding uphill first. As consistent prospecting is fundamental to success as an agent, it is important that those duties be conducted when the agent has the most energy and is fresh. According to the American Psychological Association, studies have shown that willpower is a limited resource. It is more difficult to focus on challenging tasks later in the day, when a person is fatigued.

Experienced agents establish consistent business development habits, just as we do with our "uphill first" biking rule. For example, an agent could have as a habit to not check e-mails until she has made five phone calls to follow through on leads. Most people benefit by having a reward at completion. Follow this guideline to create an anchor: "After I call five people, I will go for a brisk walk and get a cup of coffee." This simple tool makes it easier to be consistent, which creates a framework for building a business.

In the words of Robert Collier, "Success is the sum of small efforts, repeated day in and day out."

Of course, there are situations in which it isn't always possible to ride uphill first. I would still bike ride, though. The same applies to completing lead-generation activities. The purpose of the guideline is for my benefit. The beauty is that when you establish strong habits, after you've done the hard work, it is often downhill from there.

Establish lead-generation habits following the anchor guideline.

LEAD GENERATION REQUIRES DISCIPLINE AND HABIT

Oscar De La Renta believed the secret to glamour and style was discipline. He went on to say: "And if you don't dress well every day, you lose the habit. It's not about what you wear, but how you live your life." The same premise holds true with the real estate agent. The secret to success is discipline and habit. To paraphrase the words of De La Renta: "And if you don't generate leads every day, you lose the habit. It's not about what your lead-generation activities are, but how you live your life."

Agents can become paralyzed about whom to contact about real estate. It is like a fashion designer who stands in front of a closet full of clothes and accessories and proclaims there is nothing to wear!

Start with what you have. Open up the contact list in your phone and call all the people who will take your call. Look on Facebook to see who is having a life event and might be ready to make a housing change. Things to pay particular attention to are engagements, weddings, a new baby, children leaving to go away to college, or a mother-in-law coming to live. Peruse LinkedIn to see who has changed jobs or been promoted recently. The idea is to get into conversation with people.

The benefit of working with people the agent already knows is that there is a built-in trust factor. In fashion, stylists suggest that people build their wardrobe around a few classic pieces—the clothes they know and love the best. The same can be true for an agent who builds her business on a core sphere of influence. Many agents have found that a successful practice can be sustained by working with "A"-level clients. This approach also often leads to a strong referral business.

Business development for the professional real estate agent is a consistent, disciplined effort that becomes a habit. It is how these agents sustain success in the long term. It is not a "one and done." Rather, it is how they live their lives.

Establish the habit of consistent lead generation every day.

PEOPLE ON PARETO

The Pareto Principle, also known as the 80/20 rule, is the theory that the vital few (20 percent) comprise the largest portion of the output (80 percent). This means that the majority of an agent's business (80 percent) is generated from a relatively small number of people or activities (20 percent). It follows, then, that when an agent is deciding on where to invest her time and resources on lead generation, the focus should be on the 20 percent that has proven to achieve the greatest results. This is one of the key secrets successful agents apply to build and grow a business.

The most efficient way for an agent to know where his business comes from is to track lead sources and conversions. There are numerous database programs available to facilitate the process. The important thing is to do it consistently and to evaluate periodically so that you know where your business comes from and where to focus your time.

Let's use, as an example, an agent who holds open houses as her primary method of lead generation. In this case, it would be prudent for that agent to determine how many open houses she held the previous year and schedule on the calendar the next year an equal or greater number. It would not be advisable for the agent to decide to take the year off from holding open houses. This actually occurred with an agent I know. After her best year ever, she decided to switch prospecting strategies and effectively took the next year off. It was several years before she recovered the momentum lost from making that change. And guess what got her back on track? She started consistently holding open houses, Sunday after Sunday.

The Pareto Principle also applies to allied resources, staff, other agents, brokers, vendors, and others who contribute to the agent's success. It is proven that focusing time and energy on those people who contribute the greatest return on investment leads to success.

This principle applies to real estate agents, as well. Brokers will affirm that 20 percent of the agents produce 80 percent of the sales. What are you doing to assure that you are part of the select few who achieve at a high level?

Focus time and resources on the people who result in the most real estate business.

CONVENIENCE PRINCIPLE

The convenience principle is based on the premise that it is easier to sustain a habit if it is convenient to do so. For the athlete, it means running shoes and exercise clothes at the ready for scheduled workouts. For the chef, it means a well-stocked kitchen with equipment and ingredients close at hand. For the lifelong learner, it means materials stored by the coffee machine to read during her morning quiet time. And for the real estate agent, it means routinely scheduling activities for lead generation.

For real estate professionals, consistent prospecting is at the core of sustained success. Examples abound of how to use the convenience principle to one's benefit. One technique I employ is to set aside one day per week to go through my database. I do this on Sunday evenings to prepare for my week's activities. As I go through the calendar and note birthdays, home anniversaries, and so forth, I prepare a list of touches to make to past clients during the coming week. If I plan to send a card or note, I address and stamp it then and stash it in my briefcase. When I have some down moments in my day, such as waiting for an appointment, I use that time to write a quick message. All that is left to do is drop it in the mail.

In our market area, most brokers opens houses are held on Tuesdays around lunchtime. Thus, I devote that day to preview houses if I am not hosting my own listing open house. In this way, I can see quite a few homes in a short period of time, while also networking with other agents to find out what else may be coming on the market.

Viewing homes is part of my lead-generation process, as I actively think of people when I'm in a home. I use the knowledge to touch base with owners who live in the community and whom I know might be interested in what is going on in their neighborhood or perhaps considering a move to upgrade or downsize. It is more convenient to see houses on Tuesdays; thus I take advantage of that opportunity.

Getting started is half the battle for many people in lead generation. That is why a secret to success is to make it as convenient to do as possible. If it is part of your scheduled activities for the week, it becomes a routine habit. In the words of motivational speaker Jim Rohn: "Success is nothing more than a few simple disciplines practiced every day."

Establish lead-generating activities so they are convenient to complete on a routine basis.

DID YOU ASK FOR THE BUSINESS?

This is a question I remind myself of continuously. My natural inclination is that I do not want to be perceived as pushy, particularly around friends, relatives, neighbors, and associates. It is a fear of mine that when people see me, they will quickly want to turn and go in the other direction. This concern was compounded by a mortgage broker at a church our family previously attended. She was so aggressive that literally I could see the reaction on people's faces as she approached.

And yet, I am in sales, and it is my obligation to ask for the business. If I fail to do so, then perhaps customers may think that I am too busy or do not want to work with them. An example of this scenario is that my husband and I met with a CPA firm for an evaluation of our financial situation. The CPA firm provided wise counsel and offered several excellent suggestions on what we could and should be doing to improve our financial situation. And yet, the CPA never followed up. So I was left wondering, "Did he really want my business?" Perhaps he was too busy and didn't need me as a client.

In the James Bond movie, *License to Kill*, the leading lady pleads to her lover in the ballad, "If you asked me to." The words are:

If you asked me to

I just might change my mind

And let you in my life forever.

These words remind me to ask for the business. The customer just might change her mind and let me in her life. Perhaps she is waiting for me, too.

Not too long ago I was previewing homes on a Sunday afternoon when I saw a longtime friend who lives across the street. It was lovely to briefly visit and catch up. Afterward I sent a handwritten note to offer my services should she ever be in the market to buy or sell a home or know someone who is. Shortly after, she contacted me and expressed her thanks for my note and reaching out. She thought that I would be too busy to deal with homes in her price range and did in fact have a real estate need to both sell and buy. This reinforced the concept that it is important to personally ask for the business.

Another practical application is to bring listing paperwork to all appointments with sellers in the event that they are ready to sign. It means also bringing a contract packet on all buyer consultations as preparation in the event the client is ready to write an offer. And it means reminding myself as I generate leads on a daily basis: "Did I ask for the business?"

Make it a practice to ask for the business!

"SORRY SEEMS TO BE THE HARDEST WORD"

Elton John recorded this soulful song, "Sorry Seems to Be the Hardest Word." To the real estate agent, the apology often comes from a customer who decides not to use your services to buy or sell a home. People have reasons that seem valid to them at the time. Regardless of the reasons, the rejection can seem very personal to an agent; I know it does for me. The question is, what will be the agent's response? Will they no longer be friendly with the person? The approach that has the best long-term outcome for the relationship and the agent, I have found, is to take the high road.

Often, it is helpful to look at a situation from another industry's perspective. Mindy Kaling is an American actress, comedian, and writer. In her book *Why Not Me?*, she shares the story of when she found out that she was not nominated for an Emmy. Couple that with her prior engagement to be the hostess for the awards, which meant she would be reading the names of the winners. Surely if ever there was a situation in which someone had a right to take rejection personally, it was an actress whose own show was not selected.

Mindy had a choice. One option was to cancel her participation, which would have been unprofessional and potentially a public relations disaster. The other was to keep her commitment with grace and aplomb, so people would continue to think of her as being mature and classy.

To overcome her feelings of rejection, Mindy realized that as an actress she could "act as if" she was fine with the decision and visualize that outcome. Once she was able to distance herself from the actual circumstance, she was able to genuinely be happy for those who did win. To do otherwise really was no better than being a poor sport or a two year old who throws a temper tantrum.

In the case of the real estate agent, do you really want to get the reputation that you are only friends with people because they use your services to buy or sell a home? Do you want people to head in the other direction when they see you at the grocery store, the health club, on your kid's sports field only because they are concerned you will be offended if they select another agent? I choose the high road because, like Mindy, I want to live a life of grace. That is a strong foundation to build and grow a successful business. And who knows, you might be the second or third agent they decide to use who ultimately sells the house.

When people you know select another agent,
choose to accept with grace and professionalism
by taking the high road!

DAY 55

THE STRENGTH OF WEAK TIES

There is a pool of buyers and sellers ready, willing, and able to take action to move at any given point in time. The pool may be deep and wide, or it may be shallow and narrow. Yet it does exist. Even in the market crash of the Great Recession, there were still buyers and sellers in the marketplace. Experts refer to homeowners who are considering selling and officially haven't yet done so as "shadow" inventory.

Do you believe that? If you do, then you will stop waiting for the perfect client to call or walk in your office, and will instead go out and find the motivated. You will take the steps to influence people and move them along in the process if they aren't yet motivated. As an agent, you will love and appreciate the clients you have and take full advantage of the opportunities presented. Listen closely to clarify what their next real estate decision might be.

The truth is that the perfect client is rare. It is as valuable as a precious gem and meant to be treasured. The mining of leads is more like the mining for gold; there is always more debris than precious metal. This is where the value is in "the strength of weak ties" concept.

Many successful agents earn a good portion of their business from their spheres of influence. This includes family, friends, neighbors, and business associates. Agents should have a proactive and consistent method to both stay in touch with those folks as well as market their value proposition as an agent. This is the mining of the databank.

The next levels of influence are known as the weak ties. You will likely not have a direct connection with this person; it is more distant. Yet studies have found that many times this is where the opportunity lies. The visual is of concentric ripples that develop when throwing a rock into a pool of water. That's where the weak ties lie—out at the edges. It is the friend whose neighbor is thinking of putting her home on the market. It is your husband's business associate whose daughter wants to buy her first condo.

Another way to strengthen this network is to get in touch with acquaintances with whom you have lost touch. A college friend whom you haven't thought about in a while may be a gold mine of contacts. Expose yourself to other networks by attending events and social occasions that are outside your current sphere. It is in the outer circles of influence where you are more likely to engage with buyers and sellers ready to make a move.

Social media such as LinkedIn and Facebook are tremendous platforms for connecting and reconnecting. You just never know who knows whom you know!

Grow and build your network of leads by strengthening both strong and weak ties.

I SEE LIVE PEOPLE!

In the movie *The Sixth Sense*, the main character, Cole Sear, proclaims: "I see dead people." In real estate, "I see live people." I constantly think about people when I view homes. Who might want to live in that particular home or neighborhood? Which investor is in the market to take on his next property? What family is ready to upsize or what couple is ready to downsize? Which young professional is at the stage to purchase the first place to call her own?

The character in the movie goes on to explain that the people he sees are "walking around like regular people. They don't see each other. They only see what they want to see. They don't know they're dead." It is much the same way for how I see live people in real estate. They are "walking around like regular people" and often do not even know that they are ready to or need to make a move.

The professional agent develops a finely tuned sixth sense, an intuitive feeling that the time might be right for people to make a move. The couple that recently married will soon be ready to "build their nest." For the parents whose last child recently left for college, empty-nest syndrome may soon be on their minds. The investor who is ready to acquire the next rental property for his portfolio might be interested in the deal of the day.

Often the people in an agent's sphere "only see what they want to see" and don't have the vision on timing a real estate sale or purchase and the value of a particular property. People "don't know what they don't know" and that is why a good agent helps people catch the vision.

Another way to put this principle into practice is ask agents at broker's open houses: "Do you have someone in mind for this home?" If the answer is "no," encourage the agent, now that she has seen the home, to "review all of her buyers to think of who the home might would work for." This is a way to help agents "see live people" when marketing a home.

A successful agent in our area peruses the market daily for the best deal available. And when he finds it, it empowers him to contact all those people he knows who might be in the market for a "good deal." This is one additional way to "see live people" when thinking about real estate.

———————— ⚭ ————————

Think about what their real estate needs might be when you "see live people."

DAY 57

KEEP YOUR EYES ON THE BALL

Any sport with a ball will have this as one of the primary mantras. If the objective is to move the ball down the field, court, or course, then the focus has to be on the ball. Coaches will say, "Don't let the competition get into your head, but rather play the ball!"

In business, the idiom means to pay attention to the situation. It is easy to be distracted by what the competition is doing or to get involved in the minutiae of the day. The professional real estate agent knows that the game is played in her head first. She must decide that the priority is to generate leads.

The population of people in the market to buy or sell a home generally falls into three categories. One-third will immediately select the agent and move forward with the process. Another one-third will contact other agents to consider doing business with. And one-third will delay their decision.

The easy play for the agent is the low-hanging fruit of those ready, willing, and able to buy or sell a home. By all means, convert those leads. Take that ball and run with it! Remember, though, that the sweetest fruit is often the hardest to reach, which falls into the other two categories. Be sure to pursue those leads as well.

The group that selects another agent should remain in your pipeline until the actual sale takes place. I put a "watch" on the listing. In about one-third of the cases, the agent is not successful in getting the house priced to market and sold. When the listing becomes either withdrawn or expired, I circle back to the owners.

Keep in mind this is not the same as prospecting withdrawn and expired listings, as many programs advocate. That is an entirely other form of generating business. This is a ball that you had in your hands and was intercepted by another player. Just as in sports, the agent can make a comeback. Remember to honor the Realtor® code of ethics; I am not advocating going behind the sign.

The third category includes those sellers who delay their decision for myriad reasons. It also applies for buyers who haven't found a home and were in the second category; perhaps now they are ready to try another team—me as their agent! The system I follow is that every one of these potential leads has a file with an alert to follow up periodically. Every day I am in the office, I contact five of these prospects with the idea to move the ball down the course.

By going after the other two-thirds, agents can increase their lead-conversion ratios above typical numbers. Just remember, the guaranteed outcome of not trying is certain—zero conversion. Put in the effort and keep your eye on the ball for a successful outcome of customers converted to clients.

Keep your eye on lead-generation activities to convert customers to clients.

THE GOOSE THAT LAYS GOLDEN EGGS IS THE ONE THAT IS VALUABLE

The Aesop Fable is actually titled, *The Goose that Laid the Golden Eggs*, meaning it is past tense. The story is told of a couple that was not happy and satisfied with the daily provision of one golden egg per day produced by the goose. So in order to obtain all the gold, they killed the goose, only to discover that by doing so they also ended the source of their sustenance. The tale is one of greed and impatience. The moral of the story is that the old couple should have nurtured and kept the source of their sustenance alive and well.

This is first a lesson in generating and nurturing leads. In real estate, leads are like the golden eggs. For a successful agent, prospecting is an active process. Until an agent has a lead, truly there is nothing for her to do. Once the lead is obtained, like the goose, it must be nurtured in order to produce a golden egg. Both are required in order to build, grow, and sustain a business.

For many agents, the source of leads is from a rainmaker or team leader, particularly those new to the profession. After some success in nurturing and then converting leads into sales, some agents become dissatisfied, like the old couple. They think that it is the work they performed in nurturing the lead that led to the business. In these situations, seeds of discontent can grow. The rationale is that the agent shouldn't have to give as large of a portion of their commission to the lead generator.

This scenario has played out in teams across the industry. At this juncture, the rainmaker may feel the buyer agent doesn't appreciate the efforts expended to provide leads, and in a way it "kills" the relationship. In some cases, the agent learns how to generate leads and provides her own sources. Still other agents are on the proverbial search of alternative golden-egg-laying geese and move from company to company, thinking that if only they could find another one, this time they would not "kill" off the source.

Another application of the fable is that of treating referrals like the golden-egg opportunity that they are. Agents should take care of and nourish those who refer business. It is a great way to assure a steady source of future leads!

Cultivate and nourish the source of leads to your business!

DAY
59

KEEP YOUR KOOL

To be KOOL is to be a "Keen Observer of Life" according to one of the top Keller Williams trainers, Dick Dillingham. Some might call it intuition. Malcolm Gladwell refers to it in his book, *Blink*, as those people who know in an instant what is really going on. Following are a few ways in which I applied the ability to be "KOOL."

In order to best understand buyers' unique needs and wants, I discover the most by showing them homes. Rather than acting as a "tour guide," I watch and listen. This means I do not point out the kitchen and other obvious features. There are signals all around when KOOL radar is up.

An example early in my career was a young couple interested in buying a town home. We had been through about one dozen and there was no interest; the experience was just dead flat, no emotion. All of the homes were "okay," but neither of them could really articulate why they didn't like any of them. Until we were in a town home with a walk-out basement—the husband practically lit up. Thank goodness I was paying attention and didn't miss it. I probed deeper as to what about the walk-out basement he liked. He shared the story of Sunday afternoons at his uncle's home watching football in a basement like that. At half-time the kids would go out back with the adults and throw a ball around. He still had many happy memories associated with that experience. Needless to say, the couple purchased a home with a walk-out basement soon after.

In many social settings, real estate is a conversation of personal interest because almost everyone wants to know more about the market. A KOOL agent pays attention to responses and questions because often there can exist a lead-generation opportunity. One such occasion was at a business dinner with my husband. The gentleman seated next to me asked about how Zillow worked, and my opinion and experience on its validity. It turned out the couple was considering downsizing when their youngest left for college, so I was able to turn that conversation into a future listing appointment.

Being a "Keen Observer of Life" is a key to success.

Keep your KOOL by becoming a
Keen Observer of Life!

DAY

60

"JUST DO IT"

Twice my husband and I have had the privilege to visit the Mayan ruins at Chichen Itza, a UNESCO World Heritage site in Mexico. Our first visit was in the 1990s when people were still allowed to climb the Mesoamerican step-pyramid known as El Castillo. It didn't occur to me that at some point climbing the pyramid would not be an option. But a couple decades later, on our second visit, it was no longer allowed.

Like many people, I have a fear of heights. Deciding on whether to climb to the top of the pyramid presented a challenge: could I overcome my fear enough to take advantage of the opportunity? Doing so turned out to be an exhilarating once-in-a-lifetime feeling of achievement. The climb up actually wasn't as bad as I had imagined; it was the descent that proved more difficult. In retrospect, I came away with a few lessons: the experience was not as hard as I had anticipated; what I had perceived to be difficult in advance turned out not to be the challenging aspect; and the sense of accomplishment was significantly satisfying. In effect, in my mind I made it worse than it was while simultaneously diminishing the gratifying aspects. Truly, if you argue for your limitations and think you cannot do something, that is exactly what you will get.

Chichen Itza is the site where one of the most memorable Nike "Just Do It" commercials was filmed. And why the famed ad slogan resonates true for me and countless others. If I hadn't climbed the pyramid two decades ago, the opportunity would have been lost. And because I did, the experience is now stored as a great memory to draw on when future challenges present themselves.

When it comes to lead generation, the best strategy to overcome negative inertia and procrastination is to "Just Do It." Take the first step and keep in mind that once you "Just Do It," then at least you have that accomplishment to celebrate. Rarely is it as bad as imagined. Doing nothing doesn't lead to anything. Activity always generates some result.

Real estate applications have to do with situations that are challenging to deal with. Perhaps the appraisal comes in lower than the contract price, the buyer elects to void the contract, structural damage was found at the termite inspection, and so on. Clients are served best when an agent professionally faces these challenges head on with a "can do it" attitude.

The video clip of insurance executive and top salesperson Art Williams' famous speech, "Just Do It" is fantastic inspiration for anyone who needs encouragement. Successful agents "Just Do It" in business and life.

Apply the "Just Do It" motto today!

YOU KNOW HOW TO TAKE A LEAD

In a famous *Seinfeld* episode, Jerry is frustrated that a car rental company took a reservation for a car, yet didn't actually hold a car for him to pick up. This hilarious skit reminds me of what happens with agents who take a lead, yet don't convert the lead. In Seinfeld's words: "You see, you know how to 'take' a reservation, you just don't know how to 'hold' a reservation. And that's really the most important part of the reservation, the holding. Anybody can just take them."

It takes a system along with knowledge, skills, and ability to hold the lead and convert it to a sale. It is proven that what one tracks gets done, so first start with a system. My business partner, Lizzy Conroy, uses a simple spreadsheet. On it she has the contact's name, housing need, level of urgency, and the approximate dollar volume she expects to earn off of the lead. Her objective is first to take the lead and then to hold onto it until it actually is converted into a sale. No one has to follow up with Lizzy to be sure she is working her leads, although we do meet on a regular basis to coach on conversion strategies. She recognizes that each lead can be vital to her success as an agent.

Sometimes the leads are a fire hose and sometimes they are a drip. An agent starts with what he has at hand. In the words of businessman and motivational speaker Nido Qubein: "Your present circumstances don't determine where you go; they merely determine where you are." One of the lessons I have learned with experience is that, in looking back, I can see what happens in variable market conditions. Houses sell in all types of markets. The times when it is good for sellers often means that buyers don't achieve everything they want. When the market is good for buyers, then sellers typically do not get top dollar. The point is that there are transactions in all market cycles. The secret to success isn't a secret: it is to work all leads until they convert to a buyer or seller.

I recall vividly my mentor Sue Huckaby sharing a story about selling homes in the 1980s. Mortgage interest rates topped out at 18.45 percent, and at the time her husband was a congressman from Louisiana. She implored him to have the federal government do something about interest rates so that she could sell more houses. He said that she was going to have to figure out how to sell houses in spite of high mortgage interest rates. Contrast in 2017, thirty-year fixed interest rates are around 4 percent. Sue clearly did not allow high interest rates keep her from selling homes, as she went on to achieve great success with the rank of number ten in the nation a couple of decades later.

The moral of the *Seinfeld* story is no excuses—when you take a lead as a real estate agent, you hold the lead until it is converted to a sale.

Take a lead and hold it until the sale!

DAY 62

USE STATISTICS TO YOUR ADVANTAGE

The statistic "80 percent of the sale is made after the fifth contact" has been imprinted on my brain such that should I ever consider quitting before five contacts, I would soon be overruled. The numbers come from an authority that should know, the National Sales Association:

- 2 percent of sales are made on the first contact;
- 3 percent of sales are made on the second contact;
- 5 percent of sales are made on the third contact;
- 10 percent of sales are made on the fourth contact; and
- 80 percent of sales are made on the fifth to twelfth contact!

This is good news! It means that if you are persistent, your chance of success improves dramatically after the fifth try.

There is even better news, found in the classic study of sales calls made by Dartnell and McGraw Hill. It determined that:

- 48 percent of all salespeople give up after the first contact;
- 25 percent give up after the second contact; and
- 17 percent give up after the third or fourth contact.

The above data illustrates that 90 percent of salespeople give up before they even get to the point where 80 percent of the sales are potentially made. This leaves a lot of business on the table for those agents willing to put in the time and effort.

The benefit of tracking is that one knows what works and can replicate those activities that lead to success. Since becoming a residential real estate agent in the summer of 2002, I have kept a log of all the contacts I have made. First it was kept in a spiral bound notebook and later in a database program. New agents are fascinated to hear the stories of all the business I have earned through the years from the contacts I made during my first weeks as an agent. Of course, there are many touches that did not turn into opportunity. But the validity of having those numbers supports the premise that an agent can use statistics to her advantage.

There is a lot of opportunity for success—it goes to those who do not give up.

Use the power of statistics to your success at prospecting!

LEADS ARE ALL AROUND ME

The surprising thing about the real estate business is that one never knows where the next lead is going to come from. In fact, my husband reminds me of this every time one comes from an unusual place. This then makes me think of the lyrics in "Christmas Is All Around" from the movie *Love Actually*: "Christmas is all around me and so the feeling grows!" I've taken those words and changed them to: "Leads are all around me and so my business grows!" I've found that when I increase my awareness and believe that something is possible, it happens.

There are the obvious sources of leads: past clients, spheres of influence, friends, neighbors, associates, neighbors of current and past listings, open house attendees, and now the Internet. The uncommon ones are the stories that are the most memorable.

While on a business trip in California with my husband, I was taking a shuttle bus from the golf course back to the hotel. As I often do, I struck up a conversation with a lady who was seated near me and also attending the conference. It turned out that she lived in the area where I sold real estate. At the time, she was going through a divorce and planned to get her own place as soon as she returned home from the conference. Soon after, I represented her on the purchase of a town home.

Another great story comes from my business partner. She was putting out a Sunday open house sign when someone stopped and they struck up a conversation. The buyer wasn't interested at all in the house that Lizzy was holding open, but was in the market to buy. Lizzy was able to help her purchase another home in the community.

On the seller side, another story comes to mind. An agent on our team had been proactively previewing homes to stay current on the market. She had gone to see a home listed by another agent. A few days later, the owner contacted her directly. The couple was quite impressed that she would go to so much effort to be knowledgeable on the market. Needless to say, they soon made the decision to change agents and hired our agent, who sold the home for them.

These stories illustrate that by raising your awareness, you too will find that leads are all around. And when you tap into that, your business grows.

Look for leads all around you today and every day!

DAY
64

THE POMODORO TECHNIQUE®

The Pomodoro Technique® developed by Francesco Cirillo is a time-management method that uses a tomato-shaped timer. The simple idea is to set a timer for twenty-five minutes and focus on one task to completion. Then take a well-deserved five-minute break, during which time you could get up and walk around, do some stretches, or complete a quick housekeeping task. It follows how good hockey players skate: full speed, then stop.

The beauty of the built-in timed breaks is that it reduces burnout. Some people never get started because they become paralyzed by how to tackle several hours of work. Procrastination is the archenemy of the real estate agent. It is tempting to put off prospecting, particularly when you are busy. In effect, this will eventually stop the flow of business in the pipeline. It is better to consistently engage in business development every working day rather than wait until the well is dry and struggle to generate leads.

There are other strategies that employ the use of a timer. James Clear, author of *Transform Your Habits*, advocates the two-minute rule to combat procrastination. He maintains if a task can be done in two minutes, go ahead and just do it. The physics principle discovered by Sir Isaac Newton kicks in: "An object at rest tends to stay at rest and an object in motion tends to stay in motion." In this case, the object is the real estate agent staying in motion by doing something to break the inertia.

Gretchen Rubin, in her book *Better than Before*, advocates the use of a "power hour" to tackle challenging or undesirable tasks. The term "power hour" for prospecting has long been part of the lexicon for salespeople in many industries, not just real estate. The idea is to employ full engagement, to bring your full attention and focus to the task at hand.

So if it is two minutes, twenty-five minutes, or a power hour, incorporate a timer to your advantage. Whether a tomato-shaped timer or one on a hand-held device, the success key is to commit to practice. In the words of Aristotle: "We are what we repeatedly do. Excellence, then, is not an act, but a habit."

Set a timer to prospect and accomplish other key activities that lead to success.

POWER THROUGH THE DIPS

The real estate industry is like a roller coaster. The market rises and falls; what goes up also can go down. The good news is in the United States, the trajectory is generally positive in most markets. The challenge is that no one knows for sure how the market will behave the next quarter or the next year. The seasons also create natural cycles that can cause dips throughout the year.

When an agent has a buyer client who is truly an "A" client and ready to go, all is well. When the agent has a listing that is priced and positioned correctly for the market, that too is an occasion when the agent is at the top of her game. Contracts are in escrow at the settlement company and deals are in the pipeline, the phone is ringing for listing and buyer appointments—these are all signs that the agent is successful. Those are all top-of-the-roller-coaster highs, arms up in the air, a big smile on the face and perhaps even some happy screams.

Then there is the other end of the roller-coaster ride. Since real estate agents are almost exclusively paid on commission, there can often be a great deal of work to be done before any money comes in. When a transaction goes to settlement, then the fee can be substantial, yet a lot of times there is quite a bit of time in between. When the agent doesn't have anything in the pipeline, when there are no listings or active buyer clients to work with, when the phone isn't ringing, those are all the down parts of the cycle. On top of that, the real estate professional has ongoing expenses of maintaining licensure, as well as marketing and other reoccurring costs, including staff and office expenses.

It is easy and fun to be at the top; it is not so at the bottom. So how do you power through the dips? When I'm in a dip or predict one is on the horizon, I immediately get into action. Specifically, I double all my prospecting efforts. The momentum that I gain by action helps the cogs catch to start propelling me back up. The effort to get back up the other side is always greater than it is to coast down. So I know that going into the dip I don't coast, but rather I peddle and gear up so I can power through.

How do you know whether this is a dip you should push through? According to Seth Godin in *The Dip*, it is when the long-term benefits are worth the short-term pain and effort. Further, he goes on to say: "In a competitive world, adversity is your ally. The harder it gets, the better chance you have of insulating yourself from the competition."

After having experienced a few market dips in my career, I now actually enjoy the thrill of the roller-coaster ride. If I can do it, you can too!

Power through the dips in your real estate business by increasing lead-generating activities.

DAY
66

ARE YOU ALL IN?

In college I had a professor who had us visualize what our lives would be like once we graduated and entered the world of employment. The idea was that a student's full-time job in college was to learn, which meant that after accounting for classroom time, the remainder of the forty-plus hours of a typical work week should be allocated to preparation, learning, and studying. To be truly "all in" as a student meant giving everything one had to the educational experience.

To be "all in" as a real estate agent means to commit to complete consistently those activities that are known to lead to business. It is evident when an agent is working because there is production on the books, business in the pipeline, and an abundant source of leads. It is a lot like people who say they want to lose weight and get in better physical shape—their behavior is evident for all to see. They only cheat themselves. They are not fooling anyone; everyone is quite aware of what is really going on. The same holds true for real estate agents.

Being "all in" means giving the business everything you've got, even when things are difficult and even when the professional doesn't feel like it. During the Great Recession, many agents took on some challenging transactions in order to stay in business. Of those who survived the ordeal, almost all say that their business came out on the other side stronger and that as agents they are more competent and confident.

To be "all in" also means to close off all the exits. When one truly commits to the profession of real estate, there is a passion and singleness of purpose. It is like Homer's story of *Odysseus* and the seductive song of the Sirens. In order to protect the ship from the danger of the rocks, Odysseus had his men tie him to the mast so that the Siren song would not tempt him. There will always be shiny distractions that take away an agent's attention from the true activities that lead to success in the business. It is the true professional who is "all in" and stays focused.

Motivational expert Peter Lowe states: "The most common trait I have found in all successful people is that they have conquered the temptation to give up." That's another aspect of what it means to be "all in" to achieve and sustain success in real estate.

Commit to being "all in" and truly working on your business.

About the Author

Karen Briscoe is the creator of the *5 Minute Success* concept. She regularly speaks on a national and local level on the best of *5 Minute Success*. Further she is the host of the *5 Minute Success* podcast which has an amazing array of guests who achieve success at a high level in business and life. She has completed the John Maxwell Team Certification Program for Coaching, Speaking and Training.

Karen is a frequent guest on other podcasts that focus on entrepreneurial, success and motivation, as well as real estate related topics. Further, she is a contributing author to real estate media outlets *INMAN* and *Real Trends*.

Karen Briscoe is principal owner of the Huckaby Briscoe Conroy Group (HBC) with Keller Williams, located in McLean, Virginia. The HBC Group has been recognized by *The Wall Street Journal* as one of the 250 Top Realtor® teams in the United States. Since 1977, HBC Group has sold more than 1,500 homes valued at more than $1.5 billion. The team consistently sells over one hundred residential properties annually, ranging from multi-million-dollar luxury estates to condominiums and townhomes. Primary market areas include Northern Virginia, suburban Maryland, and Washington, DC.

Karen began her real estate career developing residential lots with the Trammell Crow Company in Dallas, Texas. In Northern Virginia, she worked in commercial real estate with The Staubach Company prior to entering residential sales. Karen earned a Master's degree from Southern Methodist University in Dallas, Texas and received her BA from Stephens College in Columbia, Missouri—her hometown.

She attributes her life worth living to God, her husband Andy, children Drew and Callie, her family and countless friends and business associates. Her family is actively involved at Trinity United Methodist Church in McLean, Virginia.

Karen is available to speak to your organization, group, company or association.

Want to achieve success at a higher level in business and life by investing just 5 minutes a day?

Connect with Karen and the **5 Minute Success** community!

- 5 Minute Success website: www.5MinuteSuccess.com

- **Subscribe** to **5 Minute Success - The Podcast** on iTunes, Google Play, Stitcher, Overcast and other players.

Get Social with 5 Minute Success!

- Facebook Group https://www.facebook.com/groups/5minutesuccess/

- Facebook Page @5MinuteSuccess

- 5 Minute Success Twitter: @5MinuteSuccess

- 5 Minute Success LinkedIn Page: https://www.linkedin.com/company/11064759/

Also by **Karen Briscoe**

Real Estate Success in 5 Minutes a Day:
Secrets of a Top Agent Revealed

Online Course: Commit to Get Leads: 66 Day Challenge®

Concept Authors:
Savvy Woman Success in 5 Minutes a Day
By Moira Lethbridge

Coming Soon Other books in
Success in 5 Minutes a Day 66 Day Challenge ®

Consult to Sell: 66 Day Challenge®
66 days to Focus on this Core Topic from the Original
Real Estate Success in 5 Minutes a Day

Connect to Build and Grow: 66 Day Challenge®
66 days to Focus on this Core Topic from the Original
Real Estate Success in 5 Minutes a Day

Success Thinking, Activities & Vision: 66 Day Challenge®
66 days to Focus on this Core Topic from the Original
Real Estate Success in 5 Minutes a Day

For a complete listing of other products visit:
www.5MinuteSuccess.com
Also by **Karen Briscoe**